A Heart Trimmed Christmas

A Heart Trimmed Christmas

Ruth C. Ikerman

Abingdon Press

Nashville

A Heart-Trimmed Christmas

Copyright © 1984 by Abingdon Press

All rights reserved.
No part of this book may be reproduced in any manner whatsoever without written permission of the publisher except brief quotations embodied in critical articles or reviews. For information address Abingdon Press, Nashville, Tennessee.

Library of Congress Cataloging in Publication Data

IKERMAN, RUTH C.
   A heart-trimmed Christmas.
   1. Christmas—Prayer-books and devotions—English.
I. Title.
BV45.I44   1984   242'.33   84-9258

ISBN 0-687-16804-X

The author's poems "Happy Tree," on page 20 which first appeared in *Wee Wisdom of Unity*, December 1979, and "By Another Way," on page 107 which first appeared in *Daily Word of Unity*, December 1979, are reprinted here by permission of Silent Unity.

The author's poem "On Way to Market," on page 20, was first published under her maiden name, Ruth C. Percival, in *Children's Friend*, December 1949, a publication of the Church of Jesus Christ of Latter Day Saints.

cover design and illustrations by J. S. Laughbaum

MANUFACTURED BY THE PARTHENON PRESS AT
NASHVILLE, TENNESSEE, UNITED STATES OF AMERICA

*Dedicated to
my sister-in-law Macie Louise Percival
with affection and appreciation*

Preface

A friend said to me wistfully last fall: "I wish Christmas weren't so complicated these days. I get tired just thinking about all I have to do between now and then. I wish I knew how to simplify, and I guess what I really need and want is some Christmas inspiration."

As I walked to my car, pushing a shopping cart filled with groceries for holiday cooking, I remembered her words. They remained with me through the season and undergird this book. For the purpose of this material is to help you prepare your heart and home for a happy observance of the Christmas season. All of the suggestions are meant to inspire us to live happier lives of service in the New Year.

Each chapter is centered around a theme related to Christmas—the Nativity scene, tree, toys, gifts, cooking, decorations. This is designed for individual inspiration, or it can be read aloud as part of a Christmas meditation for a church circle or club group. Each chapter also includes a project of something to make or do for home joy, and each includes a prayer.

Some of the prose and poetry deals with the joy of giving, and other pieces are concerned with the gracious art of receiving.

May we try to have humility in our hearts, homes, clubs, and churches to express the peace, joy, love, and beauty inherent in the beloved Christmas season.

Ruth C. Ikerman

Contents

1. The Nativity Scene 11
2. A Doll for Christmas 15
3. Please Tell Me a Poem 19
4. Halos for Everyday Angels 22
5. Sharing Your Christmas Cooking 26
6. The Blessing of a Homemade Gift 30
7. Christmas Flowers of Remembrance 34
8. The Shared Poinsettia 38
9. My Christmas Love Box 42
10. A Happy Secret 46
11. Holiday Finances 50
12. Christmas Balances Life 54
13. Enjoy Each Christmas 58
14. Moments with Christmas Poetry 62
15. The Facts of Christmas 66
16. The Heart-Trimmed Tree 70
17. Christmas Bazaar Blessings 74
18. Make a Christmas Heirloom 78
19. Holiday Decorating of the Ordinary 82
20. Celebrate with Christmas Cupcakes 86
21. Something *New* for Christmas 90
22. Christmas Correspondence 94
23. Silver Holly and Candles 98
24. The After-Christmas Loaf 102
25. And a Happy New Year, Too 106

1 *The Nativity Scene*

Each Christmastime I remember a happy day in travel when my husband and I were in The Holy Land. We went by car from the lovely seacoast into the hill country where grow the cedars of Lebanon.

The heavy fog of the morning had produced a thick mist so that the trees had a special spicy scent, reminiscent of Christmas trees at home. Quietly I stood beneath the wide spreading branches of one of the oldest and tallest of the trees while the years seemed to fall away. In imagination I was back to the time of the birth of Christ, and indeed to Old Testament prophecies of ancient times.

I wanted a tangible souvenir of such a lovely moment and walked over to a nearby shop. There were many elaborately carved Nativity scenes there, made from the precious wood. I was trying to decide between two delicately carved sets when I saw a little boy busily carving over in a corner of the shop.

He sat on the ground, his bare feet showing from

A Heart-Trimmed Christmas

beneath ragged baggy trousers, with his legs crossed on the sawdust, which was partially covered with cedar boughs.

Holding his whittling knife, he looked up from the piece of wood in his hands, and my eyes met his. Quickly he turned away in shyness, and then slowly raised his head again and looked at me. It was such a straightforward, honest, appealing glance that I shall always remember and cherish the moment.

He seemed so small and vulnerable on the dirt floor covered with remnants of the carving and the unused branches, and I walked over to his side. My shoes crushed the boughs so that the scent of the cedar was more intense as I reached him.

I beckoned toward the carved pieces beside him. He hesitated a moment before handing me a handful, which at first looked like pieces of a puzzle. Then I recognized the carvings as his attempts to do baby lambs, a cow, and what seemed to be a bird. It was the little bird that won my heart, for we feed them daily at home, with always a special treat on Christmas morning.

I said to the shopkeeper, "May I please buy these?"

He looked at me in amazement, as though he thought I had taken leave of my senses. "Yes," he said. "But are you sure you want them? He is very young and these are not very good."

I opened my purse and said, "They are the best he can do at this age, but I am sure he will later do carvings as beautiful as this one I am about to buy from your display case."

I asked the man to take the coins to the boy while I watched. Secretly I suppose I wanted to be sure that the lad received his wages, and I was rewarded with a happy smile.

Slowly the boy got to his feet, walked to where I was

The Nativity Scene

standing, and handed me the piece on which he had been working. It was meant to be a manger, and inside was a little stick of wood with a circle carved at the top. I recognized this as the boy's attempt to carve the Baby Jesus.

I put this into the big purse I carried and brought it home with me, where I keep it in a special little drawer in my writing room. It is not the sort of souvenir I share with others who might laugh at its awkward construction, for to me it is a thing of beauty.

The carving represents the best that the little boy could do at his present stage of development. Looking at the piece reminds me to do the best I can at my own level currently, always hoping for greater understanding and skill.

Each of us has the right and privilege of expressing the Christ of Christmas as we know him at this stage in our lives. Often I remember the sincerity of the lad at work, as I place the Nativity scene on the hall table in our home at the beginning of the Christmas season.

Humbly I bow my head and ask God to help me grow spiritually in the year ahead, and to bless the lad wherever he may be in this confused period of history. Again I pray for peace to come to the Holy Land sheltered by the cedars of Lebanon.

A PROJECT FOR HOME JOY

Find a simple Nativity scene to place on your mantel. Is there one tucked away in a cupboard which you have momentarily forgotten? If not, many are reasonably priced, including those of paper which can be assembled by children. Some Nativity scenes now come in one piece, molded of plastic, and would fit on a kitchen ledge or the top of a bookcase. When it is in place, invite the children of the neighborhood to see it, if you do not have children or grandchildren of your own. This simple activity does not call for much time expenditure, and does not complicate Christmas. Instead it leads to simplifying other activities by reminding us of the central focus of the first Christmas.

PREPARE YOUR HEART FOR CHRISTMAS

Dear heavenly Father, as we plan to observe the birth of thy Son Jesus, let it be with loving hearts filled with gratitude for thy many blessings during the year. Forgive us our neglect of those who have needed our kindnesses. Help us to make amends at this holiday season whenever possible through courtesy to those we meet in our daily activities. May it be obvious to those we deal with that we are trying to honor thee and thy Son in our daily actions, and especially at this holy season of his birth.

2 A Doll for Christmas

One of the perennial joys of the season is dressing a doll for a child. Sometimes this can become a community project, as many churches and clubs undertake to dress dolls for children who otherwise might not have them on Christmas morning.

This hobby can provide year-round handiwork for dedicated women. A shut-in of my acquaintance each year crochets caps and sweaters for such dolls to wear. She uses yarn supplied her by friends, for her pension is limited and not sufficient to cover the expenses of needlework.

One year she called me in to see the garments for dolls she had made from yarn supplied by friends. The red, blue, green, purple, gold, pink, lavender, and yellow sweaters and caps looked like a veritable rainbow as she had them arranged on her living room table.

She was to give them on the morrow to the woman who would call from the community agency charged with distributing dolls to needy children at the holiday season. My friend had given her time just so children she would probably never see could have clothing for dolls supplied by funds furnished by a men's service club.

As I looked at her handiwork I thought how neatly she had bridged the generation gap by putting her extra hours to work in this fashion so that children could feel pampered and loved at the holiday time. For in many of the homes where these dolls would go, the children were spending days in day-care centers because their mothers worked to support them. These mothers could not possibly ever find time to crochet doll clothes, but because of the loving concern of a shut-in their children might share in something of an old-fashioned handmade Christmas, such as earlier generations knew.

One young mother, raising her children as a single parent, told me with great sorrow recently: "I regret most the time I must stay away from my children on the job. Sometimes at night I am almost too tired to stay awake. In fact I often take a nap when I get them to bed, before I can start washing dishes and clothes."

She paused and waited, as if hoping I would understand before she said, "But I try to stay awake long enough to always read them a story. I hope they will remember the story hour, even though they miss so much else."

As I praised her efforts she confided shyly, "My little girl brings her doll to the story hour, and they tell me she tells the story the next day to the doll and the other children at the day-care center."

This working mother has no time for making fussy doll clothes, as her own mother had done for her. But she told me she was going to invite her little girl to come with her when she did the grocery shopping early in December. She said she would let the child look at the doll display and pick out a doll she wanted, while the mother shopped for bread and beans. She told me she was grateful that today's supermarkets provide toys for sale, as well as groceries.

I marveled at how well she had organized her limited time, and how she had indeed simplified her shopping by seeking both food and toys at the same location. And she was giving her little girl the confidence of loving companionship even though their time together was so limited.

In this new age of the working woman this mother was managing to keep alive the tradition of a doll for Christmas even as my own mother had sewed for my adored "Dorothy" a complete costume, made of my own favorite dress pattern and fabric when I was small.

And I remembered the cradle for my doll, fashioned by my father from wood from an orange crate. Because of divorce, this family had no father to help, but the mother had figured out how to make a modern cradle about which she told me. It is described in this chapter for others to use or adapt and embellish.

A PROJECT FOR HOME JOY

This mother took a green shoe box and put the lid beneath the bottom, for extra support, taping it with clear tape. Then she cut from a magazine two pictures of baby dolls, putting one at the "head" of the box, to cover the writing there, and pasting the other at the "foot" of the box to hide the pricemark. Then she bought three bright washcloths, with pink roses in the pattern, plus a matching hand towel. She used two of the wash clothes as the outer cover for a doll "mattress," stitching three sides of the cloths together with pink yarn and stuffing them with old nylon stockings which she knew would wash as well as the washcloths would. When the top was stitched shut, she had a doll mattress to put in the shoebox. She folded the third washcloth in half, again stuffing it, to make a firm headrest or pillow for the doll. As she finished stitching the top, she used the pink yarn left to form the first initial of the doll's name, using a simple chain stitch of embroidering. This initial she also inscribed on the top of the hand towel, which was to serve as a quilt. The child was entranced, and the young mother with a loving will had found a practical way to provide even in these times of inflation.

PREPARE YOUR HEART FOR CHRISTMAS

Dear God, in the busy days of getting ready to celebrate this happy season, help us remember that a precious investment of love may draw golden interest across the years. Let us learn to reach out with time, even if this represents a sacrifice. Keep us alert to opportunities for joy in our homes so that our hearts may grow to accept ever more of thy love. May we remember that it is in sharing that we ourselves grow in grace and stature as the Bible records of thy beloved Son.

3 Please Tell Me a Poem

On the bottom shelf of the bookcase in my writing room there is a little basket that contains miniature books. Children automatically gravitate to that area when they come to visit.

They like to look at the pictures, some of them so small that it is necessary to use a magnifying glass. When this game palls, they know there are larger books with regular-size type from which they can read stories.

Or perhaps they can persuade me to tell them a story. Recently they discovered that some "stories" have rhymes in them and that these are called "poems."

So it seemed perfectly natural to one little girl to snuggle against me and ask, "Please tell me a poem." The use of the word "tell" startled me at first, and then it seemed logical. If you tell a story, why not tell a poem?

She wanted a poem about a Christmas tree, and I was glad that in my files were two that I had written earlier to appear in children's magazines. There is something eternally fascinating to young and old about a Christmas tree, and so the artists had gone all out with illustrations of toys, dolls, angels, baubles, and of course a star at the top.

We looked together at the illustration for the poem called "Happy Tree":

> I love my little Christmas tree
> It always smells so sweet and clean,
> I hope it won't be lonesome for
> God's sky and all the stars it's seen.

The poem is used here in case you have need for something to read to a child—or to write in a Christmas note.

We read my second poem together about a little tree:

ON WAY TO MARKET

> Little Christmas tree on way to market
> Are you sorry to leave the hills?
> Or will you be glad for life in town,
> Center of Christmas toys and thrills?
>
> Little Christmas tree on way to market,
> You stand there bravely on the car,
> Waiting for the traffic light to change,
> Looking up as if to find a star!

Soon after the reading the child left to go home to think about decorating the family tree. After she had gone I sat quite still, remembering beautiful trees in our own home and thinking of the eternal fascination of trees. I was glad that the two had been captured in poetry to help remain in memory.

And I remembered the little "poetry books" of Christmastime which my own mother had made to entertain children in our neighborhood. Sometimes she had one in her purse at church and would hand it to a wiggly child sitting near her to keep the child amused during the sermon. How she made the book is explained here.

A PROJECT FOR HOME JOY

Choose four old Christmas cards of approximately the same size and weight of paper, each with one perpendicular fold down the middle. Cut off the signatures or erase them. Open the four cards and place them on top of one another, picture side down, and verse facing inside. Use a large-eyed needle with heavy embroidery thread to take long stitches through the four cards at the natural crease. Then refold the booklet, which will now have eight sheets, giving sixteen pages for reading or writing. If needed press briefly under a heavy book so this booklet will open and shut easily in the hands of a child. The card pictures will keep a very young child entertained, and an older child may enjoy reading the verses or drawing pictures on the blank white portions. The books are most attractive if you have enough cards for a central theme, such as four with angels, birds, or carolers.

PREPARE YOUR HEART FOR CHRISTMAS

Dear heavenly Father, we know we must become as little children if we are to truly enter the kingdom of heaven, and we are glad that we have a precious reminder of this truth at each Christmas season. Let this year be one in which all members of the family, irrespective of earthly age, have the enthusiasm and curiosity of children, exploring the wonders of this life and world. Keep us simple in our approach, and sincere in our attitudes, that there may be room in our hearts for the coming of thy Son, the Prince of peace.

4 Halos for Everyday Angels

I was stirring a batch of Christmas fudge as one of my nieces bounced around the kitchen. She went over to the towel rack and pulled out the wooden ring that holds the hand towel.

Smiling at me, she held the golden circle high over her blonde curls as she said, "Look at me, I'm an angel."

Obviously she was delighted to discover that the towel ring looked like the halos above the heads of angels she had seen on Christmas cards. Happily she expressed her delight in being thus transformed so suddenly into a Christmas angel. As I listened to her merry little voice crooning in sing-song fashion about angel halos, I reflected on her sudden transformation.

It seemed to me in that moment that she was showing me vividly that we are each to take the everyday items of our daily living and hold them aloft until they transform lives with the true angelic touch of Christmas.

Angels of Christmas come into our lives when we take a fresh look at the items that surround us daily. If we do not find Christmas in the midst of our everyday tasks, we probably will not hear the song of the angels at all. And surely we want to hear their voices at Christmastime to encourage us for the rest of the routine year.

At the heart of that message is the word "peace." Each year a great deal is written and said about "Christmas peace." Sometimes the one word P E A C E shines across an entire card as the only message. Sometimes there will be an angel nearby, the golden rays from the halo embellishing this elusive word.

Just exactly what does "peace" mean in the modern world? I had often wondered, and early in the Christmas season I went to my dictionary to determine the qualities of peace. The reference said that peace comes originally from a base word "pak-," which means "to fasten, to confirm an agreement."

How wonderful it is in life when any individual can fasten down any definite feeling of commitment. This leads on to happiness. Isn't a part of our daily tension due to rushing after things that will not be fastened down?

They elude us, and we keep on the chase, hoping to capture that elusive something called peace. Meanwhile we overlook the opportunities to make peace with ourselves. We can learn to "fasten down" our emotions and transform our anger into positive forms of energy.

Not many of us can do much about peace in the outer world, except to pray for guidance among world leaders so that there may be cessation of war and

A Heart-Trimmed Christmas

elimination of poverty. All of us, however, have it within our power to "fasten down" our own personal peace, through the acceptance of the Christ of Christmas, whose message was one of peace and good will. Before we can engage in activities leading to peace, we must first demonstrate this peace within our own hearts.

Perhaps the best Christmas gift we can give ourselves is a new determination to live in peace and harmony with those closest to us by sharing a sense of our own inner peace through Christ. As Christmas comes again, with its happy opportunities for fellowship and celebration with friends, it brings also the need for quiet moments of reflection on the power of peace in individual lives. Then quietly and imperceptibly the "halo" comes to surround our everyday activities, as peace of heart is reflected in our attitudes toward others.

A PROJECT FOR HOME JOY

This project does not call for making anything, or even for planning. Instead it suggests finding the most comfortable easy chair, whichever is furthest away from your daily duties. Put your feet on a hassock and take off your glasses, if you wear them. Let all physical pressures go from your body. Close your eyes and sit quietly for five minutes as you meditate. Another day you may be able to remain still for ten minutes, and later for fifteen, as Christmas peace flows into your heart.

PREPARE YOUR HEART FOR CHRISTMAS

Father, we seem so far removed from thy angel band as we do our earthly tasks. We lose touch with the heavenly vision because our eyes must be watching small ones at play, or our hands preparing sandwiches for school lunches. Give to us a fresh perspective of the value of our service, given in love to our families within our homes. In these days of inflation, when our work often extends into the business world, let us remember the value of honest labor. May our integrity surround us as an invisible halo of peace.

5 Sharing Your Christmas Cooking

One of the joys of each Christmas season is looking at the enticing array of foods in bakeries and markets, even though it may not be practical to buy some of everything. Likewise it is pleasant to receive food from neighbors and friends, so that there are many different seasonal taste treats.

A happy discovery in our home kitchen is that each Christmas can be used to try out new recipes. We find it easier when we concentrate on one special aspect of cooking in any one season, instead of diversifying our efforts.

There was the season when we had gone early to the apple orchards nearby and returned with boxes of the ripened, fragrant fruit. That was the year when we tried out several different recipes for apple cake, some using raw apple and others calling for cooked apple sauce. A neighbor heard of our project and produced a recipe for apple bread, so we learned a new approach.

Then there was the year we went down to the desert

Sharing Your Christmas Cooking

where grow the luscious sweet dates which make such good cakes, desserts, breads, and confections when just stuffed with nuts or fondant. For all that holiday season our kitchen was blessed with the aroma of dates baking in the oven in one form or another, reminding us of the tall fronds waving in the moonlight when we had traveled through the Suez Canal.

Through the sampling of a variety of recipes, cooking has the power of bringing far places of the world into the home kitchen. Perhaps a great-grandmother came from Europe, and her special fruitcake is repeated year after year in glorious sessions of baking which link the past with the present.

Always it is best when some small member of the youngest generation stands by to "help," even if the help may prolong the hour of the cooking. A young friend told me recently that one of the best things that happened to her when she was younger was that I had let her shell the walnuts in my kitchen on a rainy Saturday.

I had long since forgotten the incident, but she remembered it as a highlight of her Christmas. "You served me some hot punch made from some pink stuff with cinnamon in it," she told me. The "pink stuff" had been cranberry juice, which my young friend would have disdained but did not recognize when I had put some sugar and spices in it. My simple hospitality remained in her mind and heart as a happy gift of her childhood Christmases. I beamed when she brought me a luscious mince pie she herself had baked for our Christmas Eve supper.

This friend is now an attractive young matron and belongs to a church group that each year has a cookie exchange. Each member brings the recipe for her favorite cookie, typing or writing out enough copies so that each of the dozen women in the group may have her own copy to take home. She also brings a tray containing two dozen cookies, so that each of her friends can have a taste plus a sample to put in the bag provided for the purpose. When each has examined the others' recipes, the group is ready to go home to try out the new recipes, to entice their own children and family dear ones.

One of my older friends has adopted a similar tactic of her own. She experiments with new cake mixes and packs a little bit of this and a little bit of that to give to her friends. She thinks cellophane bags with built-in closure tops are the easiest way to wrap such gifts.

My friend says, "You don't have to give a whole cake or even a half cake, especially to those who live alone or have only two in the family." She cuts a generous slice of angel food cake and places it in a sandwich bag, and puts a piece of fruit cake in another. The two are then combined in a package made of aluminum foil, and perhaps tied with a red or green ribbon.

Sometimes this friend relies on seasonal paper napkins to give the decorative touch to her package. A napkin with a red poinsettia or a cluster of holly gives a cheerful note to any table. When she sends holiday cookies or candies in cardboard boxes to relatives or friends who live out of state, napkins make a soft cushion between rows of silver foil, and add to the joy of the gift as well as keeping it safer in travel.

A PROJECT FOR HOME JOY

Try something new this year in your home kitchen, working from the mixes available in most grocery stores. An angel food cake can look like a holly wreath when you add a few drops of green coloring matter to the white frosting (which may also be bought as a mix) and add some candied cherries to represent the berries. Never overlook the possibility of making instant candies by using the prepared frosting mixes, which usually tell on the box how to adjust the liquid to make candy instead of icing. Children can help in preparing such delicacies for grandparents or older friends.

PREPARE YOUR HEART FOR CHRISTMAS

Father, we thank thee for thy great goodness to us in providing so bountifully throughout the year. We are grateful for the spices that come to us from far corners of the world, making our home kitchens a fragrant part of thy great universe. Help us remember those who hunger for food so we will feel a greater obligation of citizenship to ensure that all may share in abundance. But keep us aware also of those near us who hunger for attention and friendship. May the offerings from our home kitchens always be given in Christian love.

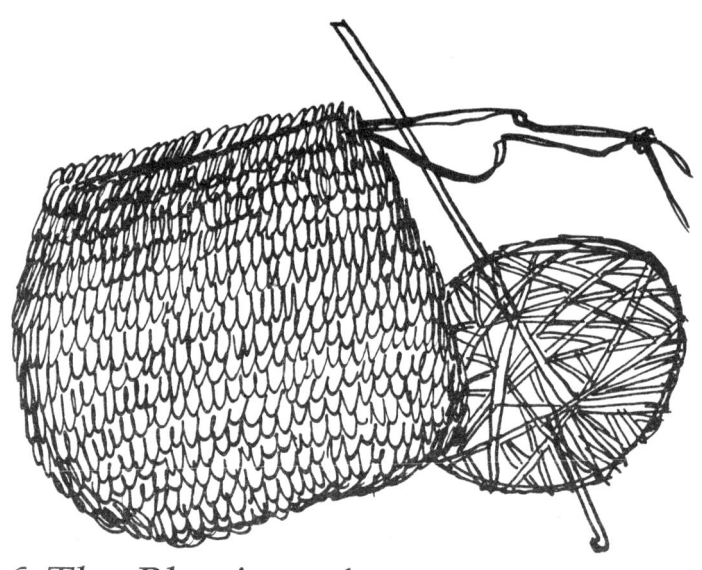

6 The Blessing of a Homemade Gift

When I was a little girl my mother encouraged me to make Christmas gifts for my grandparents, aunts, uncles, and friends. I can still remember the day when it occurred to me that it might be fun to make in secret a gift for my mother and one for my father.

How clumsy were those early efforts! I blush to remember, but nobody within the family circle seemed to mind when I handed them out at the holiday season.

Even today I can see the little handbag laboriously crocheted from colored string. In those days packages came from stores wrapped in brown paper with different colors of string for different seasons. All year long I had saved various lengths of string: green, red, purple, yellow, brown, and white, which grew dingy as I wound and unwound the ball. Finally there seemed enough to crochet this tiny bag. I gave it to my mother to use as a coin purse.

Many years later, when she was gone from this life, I found that faded little bag in her box of treasures.

The Blessing of a Homemade Gift

Obviously the item had not served its purpose of holding coins, but I have a feeling it had held the golden coins of the heart, or my mother might not have saved it for so many years.

Later on, after the first crocheting episode, I learned my "stitches" through the sampler which many little girls were taught to make. Then I could practice the various stitches on guest towels. Little did I dream that I would use those same stitches all my life, and how much joy they would add to my viewing of some of the needlework treasure in museums around the world.

As one of my first projects, I was encouraged to use blue thread to embroider bluebirds on flour sacks to be used as dish towels. We had somehow fallen heir to a package of designs, which could be traced with a pencil when carbon paper had been placed face downward on the cloth, with the pattern on top. Then the lines could be brought to life with simple embroidery stitches.

Because there were several bluebirds in the pattern package, everybody got a towel that year with a bluebird on it. Some were surrounded by pink flowers, others by lavender. Still others had bright red and orange blossoms, depending on the thread available in mother's workbasket. I know now she was also trying to teach a child the use of colors, a knowledge that grows increasingly useful in life.

Perhaps the variations on the bluebirds helped teach me to do things in quantity, for I like to make items at least in duplicate and frequently in triplicate. Now at Christmas it often seems logical to do half a dozen of the same item, almost on a personal mass-production basis. It saves time in figuring out new patterns, and often the aprons or Christmas hotpads may be puchased in quantity, so less shopping is involved.

In any event the practice of making a homemade gift

A Heart-Trimmed Christmas

for friends and families has remained with me across the years. It brings endless delight in planning ahead, and needlework is good therapy for natural nervousness in tense moments of indecision or family worry.

As with most habits, this custom just grew, and I was not really aware of it until a close friend said: "If you ever give me a gift at Christmas which doesn't have some handmade touches on it, I'll think you don't love me any more. I look forward to your homemade gift each year."

Usually these gifts were so simple I marveled that she even remembered—perhaps just a cross-stitched initial on a napkin. Her delight could not be because the work was flawless, for it was not. Often the gift is much less professional looking then a table mat from a store, but I have fun putting my friend's initials on a plain piece of linen to put beneath her plate and cup, and visualizing her using it at mealtime.

Making several gifts alike enables me to make the best possible use of available material, and save time in cutting and stitching. Sometimes even cutting is not necessary, if I can use a terry towel to sew onto a plain band for an apron. Often during the year the colorful towels are on sale in a favorite store, just begging to go home with me and hide until they emerge as aprons.

A year-round project of working on some homemade gift adds zest to the seasons. Many are the variations of such a gift, but the blessings continue to grow and multiply, for only you, yourself, can offer any individual something you have made with your hands as a gift of love from the heart.

A PROJECT FOR HOME JOY

A young family plagued by inflation made a rich gift to our home through the truly "handmade" gift, which

The Blessing of a Homemade Gift

used one piece of typing paper and colored pencils. The father placed his hand in the center of the paper, while the mother traced around it with a black pencil. Then she placed her hand inside his larger one, while he traced hers with a blue pencil. Then the children, according to age, added their hands, each outlined with a separate colored pencil. The legend said in the father's handwriting: *We all wish you a blessed Christmas.* They made it so, for we cherish this memorable handmade gift.

PREPARE YOUR HEART FOR CHRISTMAS

Father, we acknowledge that our talents come from thee, and we thank thee that each of us has a different contribution to make to life itself. Let us be generous in sharing with those closest to us, that they may feel thy love expressed through our actions. Help us expand that circle of fellowship by caring for those we meet in our daily routine, giving of our best selves in the earning of a living and making of our lives. May we grow in spiritual grace so that we may have more to share with others.

7 Christmas Flowers of Remembrance

It was a Christmas when sorrow had to be pushed back in the heart and somehow kept from intruding on the joys of others. During the year death had taken two precious members of the family. Their presence had always been a blessing, particularly at the beloved Christmas season, and it was hard to face this first season without them around the tree.

Walking away from the people gathering in the living room around the tree, I went outside to the garden at the sunset hour of Christmas Eve. There I felt it would be easier to quietly ask God for strength to be poised on the happy day of Christmas with all its usual festivities.

As I walked along the cedar hedge bordering our California home, I noted a piece of something white, facing the house in a sheltered spot. Naturally I thought it might be a piece of scrap paper blown there by the autumn winds.

The winds seemed late this year, even as summer had lingered on in what "oldtimers" were calling "most unusual weather." But even this did not prepare me for the surprise when I stooped to pick up the supposed paper.

I found with amazement that this was no inanimate object, but a living flower. I held in my hand a white Easter lily blossom, from the plant that had been sent to us at Eastertime, following the death of loved ones. Only one blossom of white was in bloom, but obviously because of the unseasonal weather, this plant had decided to blossom again at Christmas.

Humbly I picked the one Easter blossom, took it into the house, and went in search of my favorite vase, a crystal and silver one just right for one flower. I placed the lily beside the Bible, and opened it to the Christmas story.

What a blessing it was to have this visible evidence that Christmas and Easter had been integrated in nature. Surely then they could be joined in my heart.

Without Christmas there would be no Easter, and the lily had returned to tell me so in all its purity and beauty. Was it just a special combination of weather circumstances that had made this evident? Or did God know how much I needed special assurance this particular season? I chose to believe the latter. Such a blooming may never happen again in our garden, but it does not need to happen again. Now I know that Easter and Christmas are a unity, a part of the blessed gift of God through his Son, with the promise of life eternal to those who accept and believe.

Christmas comes each year, whether we are in a happy mood or a sad one, and sometimes it takes years to recover from sorrow, which seems particularly heavy at the holiday season. I often think back to the weekend of world mourning observed at the time of the violent death of the late President John F. Kennedy. My husband and I were in Australia on a tour that weekend and felt inexpressibly sad at the turmoil caused in hearts all over the world. With great courtesy the Australian people offered to us their sympathy on tour buses and in hotel dining rooms.

At the airport as we were returning home, I heard my name called just as we were about to leave for the boarding area. Running toward us were three young teenagers—the son of one of our hosts, and two of his friends. They had gone out into "the bush" that morning in search of the Christmas flower, which covers the hillsides on the warm Australian Christmas days. (Often families there celebrate the holiday with outdoor picnics.) I had expressed interest in the plant, and these lads had gone out early this November Saturday to look for a sprig. They handed it to me along with a safety pin to fasten it on my coat.

For miles across the sea, I enjoyed the red blossom. I still think of it as a badge of courage, which we all need at times of sorrow. It was cherished the more because it was given with such youthful and loving enthusiasm by students my husband and I had only recently met. The Christmas corsage comforts me in memory, and while the Australian Christmas bush flowers have long since faded, I visualize them blooming on the hills when my friends observe their family Christmas in happiness.

Christmas flowers of remembrance can link sorrow and joy together, when we try to comfort the living with what is available from our homes and hearts.

A PROJECT FOR HOME JOY

It may seem strange to use the word "joy" in connection with this suggestion. Yet I think if you will take a family plant which you enjoy and add a festive touch to it for Christmas, it may take away some of your private sorrow. Tie a red bow at the top of a fern or piece of greenery. Or wrap a white towel around the brown pot that holds the blooming African violet a loved one formerly tended. Move your chosen plant close to a family photograph. Shed a tear if you need to, but keep the family circle intact in an atmosphere of beauty, and you will revive memories of happier years. Christmas can be a link between the here and the there of earth and eternity.

PREPARE YOUR HEART FOR CHRISTMAS

Dear heavenly Father, it is hard to face the joyous season when sorrow remains in our hearts. Please give us a special portion of thy grace so that we may remove the memories of pain and hurt and separation, and return to glad memories of shared family happiness. Bless our sorrows to our future use, so that we may be enabled to serve thee better, even as we learn to know ourselves better. May we face up to our need of thee and of others, and become stronger to help those we meet in the way who need help in carrying their special burdens.

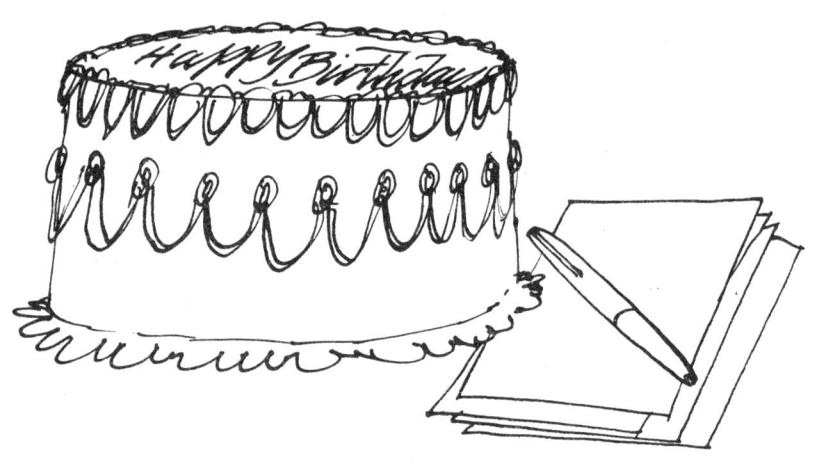

8 The Shared Poinsettia

He was sitting in a chair in the hallway nearest the nurses' desk as I entered the convalescent home. Usually he was staring at the doorway, watching for me.

But today his eyes were focused on a red poinsettia plant. Its green leaves contrasted against the golden foil around the flower pot.

His face lit up with a happy smile as I said, "Hello, Father." With one finger he pointed toward the Christmas flower, and I said, "It is beautiful."

He beckoned to me and I went closer to hear his failing voice. "It is mine," he said, "and I told the lady to put it out here where everybody could see it."

Glancing around, I saw that it was indeed the first of the nursing home Christmas decorations. Who, I wondered, had brought it to him? He told me that it was the same lady who had always taken a plant to him and my mother on the first Saturday in December. That way

The Shared Poinsettia

they could enjoy its beauty together in the family home all the holiday season.

In memory I could see the earlier plants on the kitchen table by the sunny window, towering above a fresh pan of gingerbread. This was Father's first Christmas alone, since Mother's death, and away from the home where they had lived more than seventy years of their married life.

"I didn't expect this flower this year," he told me, "but the lady remembered and came all the way here to the rest home to give it to me."

He wanted to know if I would write her his thanks, and I said I would call her the minute I was home, to thank her for this happy moment in my father's lonely Christmas.

Father confessed, "I told her there wasn't room for it on the tiny table in my little room with its narrow bed, and so I thought she ought to take it home with her. But she insisted it was mine to keep. So I asked the nurses if I could put it on the ledge by the big desk."

Permission had been granted. Now he walked from his room, holding carefully to the side rail along the hallway, to take a look at his flower twice each day. Meanwhile other patients gathered near it in their wheelchairs to see if new green petals had turned to Christmas red.

My own heart had been cheered when I first saw the plant as I entered on my own visiting errand. I had slowed my steps to take a closer look at this happy symbol of the season. Now I was indeed comforted as I heard the lovely story of the loving gift of remembrance from a faithful friend.

How many happy memories of the past were revived for all those in the home by the sight of the beautiful plant, which blessed the hours of this present sad season. The shared poinsettia lavished its beauty on the strong and the weak, encouraging all to live courageously in the New Year. This attitude was made possible by the simple gift of a red flower from a friend who remembered. Her loving act blessed an entire nursing home. She recognized that this was a changed season in the life of my father, but she brought something as a symbol of the fact that some things, such as friendship, need not change.

Outer circumstances of living may be changed, and we may need to learn to change with them. But there are things we can do to comfort ourselves and others in facing the challenges of this earthly world of change.

Admittedly this is hard to do at the happy holiday season, but we can make it more bearable for ourselves and others by keeping in mind the central message of Christmas. We can realize anew that Jesus was born into the world to bring a message of peace and love from God the Father, and that by accepting him we become brothers and sisters in the great human family of God.

This realization calls for an expression of responsibility on our part in trying to serve those who need help. Perhaps it is possible to arrange a busy schedule to make a rest home visit. If this is not feasible, perhaps a card can be mailed. It does not need to be expensive—in fact a postcard can be propped against a window, whereas a card in an envelope often must be opened by an aide, and then may be returned to the envelope and not seen again. Christmas offers opportunity to try to serve others with beauty of spirit.

A PROJECT FOR HOME JOY

Try to think in terms of little things instead of big ones. Can your friend in the nursing home still write? Then an inexpensive pen will bring joy for an entire year. Can you offer even one afternoon a month to go into the room and write letters for one who can no longer write? Or would you rather bake one cake a month and take it to the recreation supervisor for use at the monthly birthday party? Infinite are the needs that can be met by comparatively "little" services which mean much to those now removed from the mainstream of life.

PREPARE YOUR HEART FOR CHRISTMAS

Father, it is hard to have conflicting emotions at the holiday season especially. We remember joys through our sorrows and our tears, and we need help in making the smiles remain in our eyes and come to the faces of those we love who are now incapacitated. Let us know that thou art in the good days and those which seem to us to be the bad days, and that all balances out in thy great plan of goodness for the lives of all thy children. Help us to serve thee with love, remembering that we find thee close to thy needy children.

9 My Christmas Love Box

Once upon a Christmastime I had taught a little neighbor girl how to write her letter to Santa Claus. Now she herself was a young mother with two small children, and living far from "home."

So I looked around our house to see if there was something I could send her without stretching the family budget, and because shopping time at this late date was limited. Little did I think that morning that I was establishing what has become my "Christmas Love Box." For it is surprising the things that can be discovered in any household when love is the motivating power of the search.

The first possible gift for my friend and her young family which I encountered in our home was a plastic ornament which had been a party favor for me. It could be mailed at little expense and without the danger of breakage, and the blue and gold design would enhance any table. Besides the blue was the shade of my young friend's eyes!

My Christmas Love Box

Next I thought about her children and wondered if there was anything at all available in our home for them. Suddenly I remembered the two dolls, a boy and a girl, which I had been unable to overlook during a hot summer "special" when they were offered as a premium at my favorite shopping market.

Sure enough, the dolls were still in a sack in the cupboard, but they looked forlorn without blankets. Quickly I hemmed two pieces of flowered flannel found in my workbasket.

In my bookcase I saw two alphabet books purchased at a sale when I could not resist the entrancing animal pictures. I had thought that perhaps some child would discover them on the shelf, but they could be replaced and these sent on ahead to say "Merry Christmas" to my friend's children in their new home.

Fortunately there was a duplicate copy of the perennial favorite "The Night Before Christmas," since I can never pass up the lovely new editions which appear each year. Now there are available coloring-book editions, and even versions with stickers, to accompany the prose with which Clement Moore entertained his children more than one hundred years ago.

Happily I placed the items in the sturdy box in which a new kitchen pan had arrived for me earlier in the week. I took the box to the post office on my first trip to town. As I looked at the address of my young friend and her family I could sense her loneliness in a cold state far from her birthplace. My own heart was lighter as I visualized her opening a package from her "growing-up-neighborhood," and then I dismissed the matter from my mind.

Imagine my delight when in the first mail of the New Year there was a letter from my friend, written on lined tablet paper! Precious were the words which warmed my heart: "Just a note to thank you for all the gifts you sent the kids. Sister really enjoys the books and even though the baby can't understand them he loves looking at the pictures. The two dolls are really adorable. Sister calls them 'Brother and Sister,' just like herself and her brother. They both get a kick out of those, and the two blankets are always in use. She tucks her dolls in bed and uses the blankets for their cover. It's really cute to watch. Or else she'll try wrapping her own baby brother up in them, but he doesn't care for the idea at all.

"The little Christmas tree ornament is really cute, too, and Sister made me hang it on the tree as soon as she saw it. I just wish you could see the children having so much fun with the things you sent. Our Christmas was nice, but I missed home and everyone. It means so much to a person on a special holiday to be with all the ones they love. I just want to say 'thank you' again and tell you how happy your love box made the kids when they opened their gifts."

She had called it a "love box," and out of a full heart had written me. It was with a full heart that I read her beautiful words, expressing real feelings of loving gratitude.

How easily I might have missed this contact, thinking that what I had in the house was too little to offer. I resolved this would not be the case again, for I would establish a year-round "Love Box" into which to place possible gifts. Over the years I have found that items in this box are useful for community giving, even when I do not know the young families personally.

A PROJECT FOR HOME JOY

Find a place in a closet or cupboard where you can keep your Love Box. Maybe one of the boxes in which your

My Christmas Love Box

own Christmas gifts arrived can do happy double duty by serving throughout the year as a receptacle for items which can later be shared. A young friend who established this plan a year ago told me of the pleasure she and her children had in emptying the box in the summertime when the call went out from the Sunday school for toys and clothing to take to a mission school in Baja California. The children learned the joy of giving when they started using the Love Box.

PREPARE YOUR HEART FOR CHRISTMAS

Our loving heavenly Father, we embrace this Christmas season as a fresh opportunity to offer love anew to the children of all ages with whom we share the Christian faith. Grant to us the ability to make happy memories for others, even as we learn to share from that which thou hast given to us. Keep us aware of that which we have to offer in the way of encouragement through kindly acts, which do not need to rely on heavy expenditures of a material nature. Let us never withdraw from life, but always share with others the life abundant.

10 A Happy Secret

Early in the New Year a very special letter arrived in our home from England. It described a Christian family's Christmas observance and revealed a happy secret about a meaningful holiday.

This happy secret involves caring for others, an act that can be learned early in life, as the letter indicates. The mother wrote with simplicity and charm to warm our hearts and give us one of our happiest holiday moments involving correspondence.

"We had a very happy Christmas. I was quite amazed to discover how much our son understood at two years old. He recognized the animals in our Christmas crib and 'Baby Jesus' and 'Mother Mary.' He picked out Mary and the Baby Jesus on every Christmas card.

"One night when I picked him up from his bed, he said, 'Poor Baby Jesus, no bed.' Another time, when he was looking at a Nativity picture, he remarked, 'Poor Baby Jesus, no teddy bear.' His teddy bear goes to bed with him every night.

A Happy Secret

"It just shows how even very young children can understand more than we might imagine. He evidently realized what we sometimes forget, that a manger was a poor sort of crib for any baby.

"We are so used to seeing the Baby Jesus in a manger that we tend to think of it as the place where he should be, but our son knew he ought to be in a bed, and that he lacked the comforts which our children take for granted. What a lot there is to be learned from small children!"

Her letter reminded me of the joy we all may have at the Christmas season when we return to the simple faith we had as children. Then as adults we may continue to accept the blessings that belief in the Christ Child brings into our daily lives.

Such belief involves caring for others, even as Christ has cared for us. Surely some of the joy of Christmas comes in remembering those who are often forgotten during the busy year. There is pleasure in the gesture of sending a nosegay of holly into a room at a rest home and seeing the happy face of the recipient light up as she looks at it on the bedside table.

The same rewarding feeling is available every month of the year if some simple treat can be planned for such persons. Giving an inexpensive calendar in January is one simple way to start a habit and avoid after-Christmas letdown.

The pleasure children get from their toys at Christmas remains a happy memory to adults through the year. The memory can be made sweeter by arranging to take a neighbor child to a concert or the circus.

The reason Christmas adds to the year-round joy of the heart is that it encourages individuals to get out of their own routines and think of the lives of others.

Naturally there is a letdown when the mind returns to the same old routine, but it does not have to be that way.

The little boy whose mother wrote the letter had learned the happy secret of putting himself in the place of another—this time the Baby Jesus, whom he saw represented in the crib and on Christmas cards. With childlike faith, adults can enlarge on the little boy's remarks by getting over into the realm of action in following through on good resolves which involve helping others. And the first essential is to care enough to make a Christian effort.

A PROJECT FOR HOME JOY

Let the children help in clearing away the Christmas clutter. It is always fun to help decorate, but not so much fun to put away the decorations; yet this is a habit which must be cultivated. While doing it, there is opportunity to think of sharing with others. Are there toys from last year with which the children will part, now that they have new ones? With the Christmas spirit intact, is there a doll or a book or a ball that they will want to take to Sunday school for a mission project? Maybe some of the plastic holly or mistletoe does not need to be saved for your home decorations next year and can be used in a bouquet for the church school library. Sharing learned at home can be a great gift to your children, for it is a happy secret of wholesome, abundant living.

PREPARE YOUR HEART FOR CHRISTMAS

Father, accept our thanks for thy loving concern for us and our dear ones. Help us enlarge that circle to include the world, as did thy son Jesus, whose birth we

A Happy Secret

celebrate each Christmas season. Make us mindful of the little ways in which we may show our concern for others to whom our kindnesses may loom large on the lonely pathway of life. We thank thee for thy blessed presence on our earthly pilgrimage and for thy ever-present concern, on which we may rely. From this reassurance may we gather fresh strength for future service.

11 Holiday Finances

I was waiting outside the pay telephone booth to make a call to a friend who had moved to the city we were passing through on our vacation. The young woman using the telephone ahead of me suddenly emerged from the booth, her eyes so filled with tears that she did not see me.

Obviously she was greatly distraught, and her embarrassment was great when she swung to the right and collided with my purse, which I had put up to shield my arm and face. "Forgive me," she said, "but I've just had the worst argument with my family, and I don't know what to do next."

I said, "I am a stranger here, passing through, and I doubt that I could help at all, but if you want to tell me about it briefly, I'll listen."

She stopped in her tracks and wiped her eyes and said, "Thank you, but it's about money and how to pay for Christmas gifts for my children, and buy a turkey for the dinner."

Holiday Finances

What I wanted to do was to reach into my purse and hand her a bill, but I felt what she needed more than anything else was a fresh spurt of self-confidence. So taking her hand in mine, I said, "You look like a fine young mother to me, and I am sure you will be able to figure out a way to handle it best for your own family."

She held on to my hand for a while and said, "I'm so glad you were here. I'm nearly desperate. My mother-in-law doesn't know the first thing about the financial problems of this generation, and my husband and I are really trying to do the right thing. He works so hard, and I do some typing of term papers at our home."

Again I said, "You will make out all right. Try to pray about it, and keep your temper, if you can."

She gave me a rueful smile as she went to her car, and then she came back and said, "Wherever you spend Christmas, I hope you have a merry one."

Her wish stayed with me throughout the whole season, and I put that young woman, nameless to me, on my prayer list for holiday happiness. I was sure she had a point about the lack of understanding between the generations, but I also knew that she herself could not understand the financial problems of the earlier generations.

At Christmastime the matter of finances comes into sharp focus and often points up the differences in the ways people value money and in their habits of thrift. Sometimes all of us seem to be like Alice in Wonderland, who confessed to having to run twice as fast in order to stand still.

Yet there are ways to plan ahead for Christmas finances, as has been proved by some of my thrifty friends. One of them has what she calls her "Holiday Cupboard," in which she stores such baking staples as

A Heart-Trimmed Christmas

flour, brown sugar, white sugar, a can of powdered chocolate or cocoa, and candies to sprinkle as decoration.

"My income is so low at this point in my life that if I waited until December I could not buy all the ingredients I need for the baking I love," she told me. "So I plan ahead and buy one thing each month for that shelf."

Inside tin cans with lids which protect from moisture or pests, she stores such items as raisins when she can find them at lower prices. In other cans she keeps nutmeats from walnuts and almonds from trees of friends, or found at bazaar sales. She prepares her shelves for the making of holiday treats for friends.

Another friend, who always writes me a Christmas letter, uses special stamps—not Christmas stamps, but ones which have appeared through the year. When I told her how pleased I was to see the picture of a poet on my envelope and to have her note referring to a poem of mine, she said, "I saved that stamp for you."

Then, with remarkable candor about her finances, she told me, "I wouldn't be able to send notes now if I didn't plan ahead for the necessary postage. It may sound silly to you, but I save in a special envelope two stamps from each of the batches I buy during the year, which is usually once each month. That way I am sure of at least twenty-four stamps for two dozen letters for friends."

Her notes now seem to me even more precious than before, as I reflect on her loving wisdom and her wish to keep in touch in spite of limited finances. It takes humility of spirit, and reduction in pride, to deal with such comparatively small matters as saving two postage stamps a month, but the end result is keeping the Christmas circle of fellowship intact.

Christmas offers an opportunity to take a fresh look

at values and goals which can encourage thrift, and to think of others in loving Christmas gestures of correspondence.

A PROJECT FOR HOME JOY

Encourage each member of the family to make a monetary gift to some person or special cause. Strange as it may seem, family funds appear larger when you are able to give some money to a good purpose. Remembering my friend and the postage stamps, I buy little books of stamps to be used by patients in a mental institution, who may be well enough to write home but whose funds are limited. This sharing makes me more grateful for the health to be at my typewriter in my writing room.

PREPARE YOUR HEART FOR CHRISTMAS

Dear God of the abundant life, forgive us for thinking of our limitations, and help us to know that there is ample supply for all our needs in thy great universe. We know that thou art more willing to give than we are to receive, and we need thy help in cultivating a sense of peace about our physical and financial needs. Give us grace to share from whatever we have in our present financial state. Let us grow in knowledge and willingness to give generously of ourselves, as we share thy good gifts.

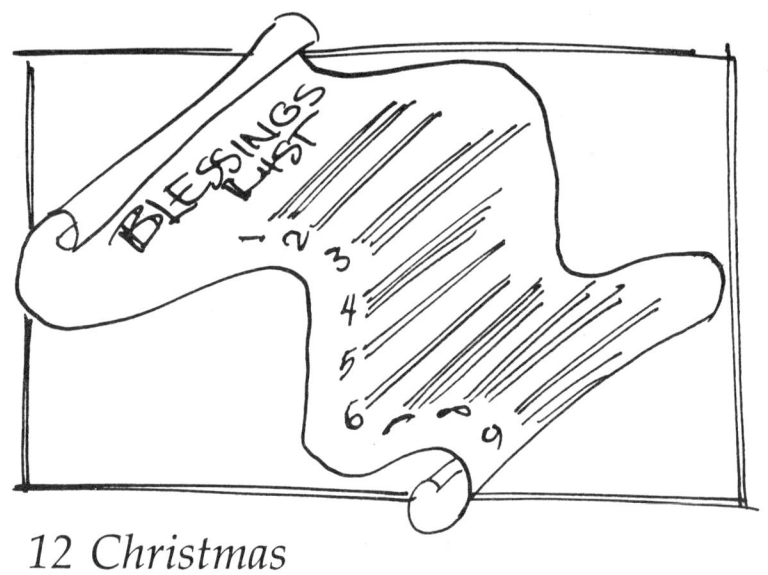

12 Christmas Balances Life

It is the happy custom in my former neighborhood for those of us who lived side by side to get together for a Christmas breakfast sometime during the holiday season. The group is not large, just five women, who shared life's joys and sorrows in busy days of routine for almost twenty years.

Now one has moved into a mobile home, another retired from business, a third travels often to visit her children, a fourth keeps to her busy life as a dietician, and my own days seem to center around typewriter and kitchen. Maybe we don't hear from one another often now, but we live fairly close geographically with freeways available, so we make a yearly effort to get together one morning each December.

Sometimes the meeting is in a home, and other times at some restaurant where we can order coffee and sweet rolls, so no one has to become involved with dishes or decorations. What we want is restored fellowship through the simple magic of some good talk. The breakfast is a happy occasion and seems to set the mood for the rest of the season, as we share again what the year has brought.

If this has been an outstandingly good year for some of us, with promise of special joy at the holidays, then surely this is the time to share compassion and kindness with the one who has known great sorrow as the year progressed. We become as one as we talk, and Christmas seems to level the year, permitting us to strike a balance in our hearts.

Even as we mention the events in the outer world, we sense what has happened within the heart as one neighbor tells us of welcoming a new grandchild, another of suffering with a child who was divorced, and a third of learning to manage with a reduced budget.

On the other side of the ledger is the planned trip to visit a daughter living in a foreign country, the opportunity for advanced professional study, and an exciting new creative project.

On one such occasion, in a reflective mood, we wondered why the group persisted, and why we had merged such neighborly friendships when we were such different women, with varied problems.

One friend solved the puzzle by saying, "This is the group I can ask for favors and know they will be granted if at all possible." It was true—we had each asked another for help in many instances. Always the neighbor had responded to the best of her ability and with frankness.

Sometimes the asking had been for a tangible gift, such as a cup of sugar, or some butter to add to icing for a birthday cake. At other times the gift had been a shoulder on which to sob out worry over a child's illness, or a strong arm at time of death in a family.

There is opportunity at Christmastime to reflect on

A Heart-Trimmed Christmas

such blessings, and this reflection is at the heart of our holiday meeting of former neighbors. At the beginning of our coffee we join hands and spend a few moments in silence until one member says, "May God bless each of us and all those dear to our hearts that we may serve him better in the year ahead."

Is there a better way to face up to the balance afforded by the coming of Christmas than to ask a blessing on our current lives, no matter what has come into them in this past year?

Only then are we prepared for a new year of service. The coming year may not take us to some glamorous distant city or country, but it surely will offer opportunities for joyous fellowship and service in our own neighborhood.

A PROJECT FOR HOME JOY

Take time to sit down and make another list in this month of lists—gift lists, food lists, decoration lists, appointment lists. Head this "My Blessings List." Start with the fact that you are able to write such a list and have the strength and ability to hold pencil or pen. Take it from there, and you will be surprised how far the blessing list will stretch. Write it in shorthand, if you choose, so that nobody else will know what items form your thanks. This may be your own special abbreviation for words, not necessarily a recognized form of business shorthand, and it can be fun to devise such a personal language. Sometimes I use the first two letters of a word to remind me of what I meant by the phrase. True Christmas happiness rests on thanksgiving.

PREPARE YOUR HEART FOR CHRISTMAS

Dear God, we thank thee for the blessings of friendship in our lives, and that Christmas comes again when we may strike a balance in the year fast drawing to its close. We are grateful for all that thou hast given us across the changing years of our lives, and yet so much remains for which we would still ask thee. Sometimes we grow self-conscious in asking, thinking that our requests may seem repetitious. Help us to know anew that thou art more willing to give than we are to receive, and let our lives overflow with thy grace.

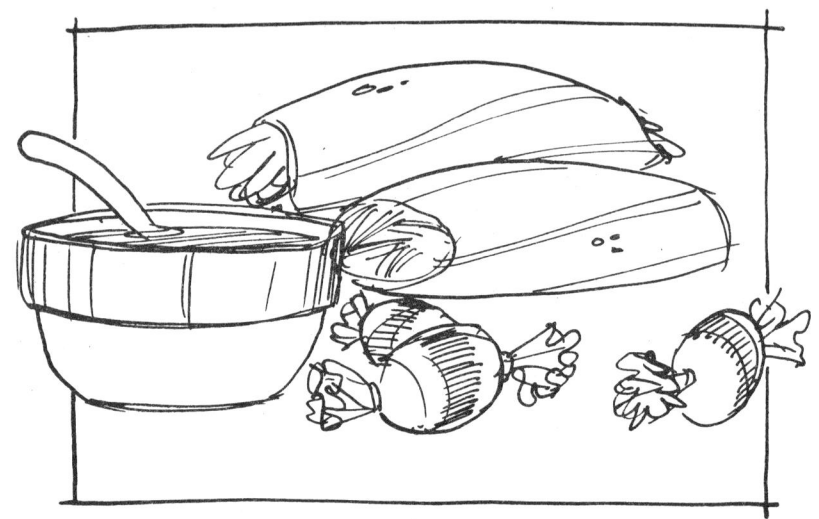

13 Enjoy Each Christmas

Many beautiful legends, carols, and customs center around the happy season of Christmas. Each country seems to contribute its best talents of music or treats from the family kitchen in devising ways to observe this holiday.

It is the custom in the Southwest, where my husband and I live, for Mexican friends who have migrated north from their country to keep to the tradition of tamales for supper on the Eve of Christmas. So we are usually prepared for the fact that at least one of the times the doorbell rings on that evening, we will see at the doorway the children of a Mexican family, bringing us this delicious treat.

These tamales include not only the familiar ones, with meat and sauce inserted in the corn or maize outer wrapping, but also many made from recipes for the sweet tamale, which serves as a holiday confection. We look forward to this annual treat, and think of customs in other countries also.

Enjoy Each Christmas

We can visualize our young friends in England enjoying their "Christmas snappers" following dinner, complete with a luscious plum pudding. The snappers seem to have almost an international following now, as children pass along the little paper envelopes or sacks, which, when popped open, contain some miniature toy or piece of candy or holiday cake.

Then there are the groups of carolers who come to the doorway singing the enduring melodies of hope and love. And it is fun to go to the door and distribute some homemade candies or share cookies with them.

In recent years this custom of singing of carols has spread to many shopping malls. Often down the center of the big walkways dividing the two sides of the shopping areas there will be a long row of Christmas trees. A sign tells which school in what town decorated each individual tree. One group may have chosen a Victorian theme with white angels and embroidered pillows as decoration, and another may have used brightly colored fabrics with holiday designs.

It is now possible to buy fabrics, in yard-goods stores, which are already printed with reindeer, snowmen, or holly wreaths. All that is needed to make enchanting ornaments for the family tree is to cut around the Christmas pattern, stitch, and fill with stuffing.

In this mobile age when business and military commitments take many families from one end of the country to the other, it is hard to hang onto the box of cherished ornaments. So easy-to-make and hard-to-break ornaments are in order, and enterprising artists have found a way to fill this need.

Displays of elaborately decorated Christmas trees serve as wonderful fund raisers for charity in many parts of the country. Clubs which sponsor them find that people love to come to admire the trees with their dazzling ornaments, and spend much time in picking out a theme for the year.

All of these items and events are a joy to experience, but sometimes they tend to obscure from our vision the true meaning of Christmas. The facts of the original event were simple, and not complicated as many of the festivals of today.

Efforts are made sometimes to recreate the simplicity by having pageants depicting the sequence of events. Figures as large as deparment store mannequins may be expertly costumed and used in life-sized displays.

A Christian retirement community in our area attracts many visitors each night in the week before Christmas as families drive through to admire the manger scene, complete with live lambs on the green lawn. Spotlights highlight the colors of the jewels on the headdresses of the wise men. And the shepherds' clothing contrasts with the silk and satin hues of the kings.

All such attempts to help people visualize the first Christmas are good in keeping its eternal message alive in the space age. Such exhibits and trips should be enjoyed with friends and family as Christmas comes again.

A PROJECT FOR HOME JOY

Resolve to enjoy together whatever is the newest attempt to recreate the first Christmas. This may be a new exhibit at a shopping center, the carols of the student chorus at a nearby college, or a long delayed visit to an art exhibit in a nearby town. It is so easy at the holiday season to put off "until next year" the seeing of the beautiful objects arrayed in Christmas displays. Next year merges into the next, and the children grow up and are not available for such family fellowship.

Enjoy Each Christmas

Make this the year for a happy Christmas outing together. One of the advantages is that all ages can enjoy such festivities, and many of them are offered without charge.

PREPARE YOUR HEART FOR CHRISTMAS

Father, we are grateful for the enduring truths and joys of the Christmas season, and for the many ways in which it is observed throughout thy wonderful world. Give us guidance in the use of our time that we may enjoy to the utmost what is available to us in our own communities, churches, and through the music of radio and the performances of television. Help us keep alive the great traditions of this season, which observes the birth of thy Son, and put peace and love into our actions in the New Year.

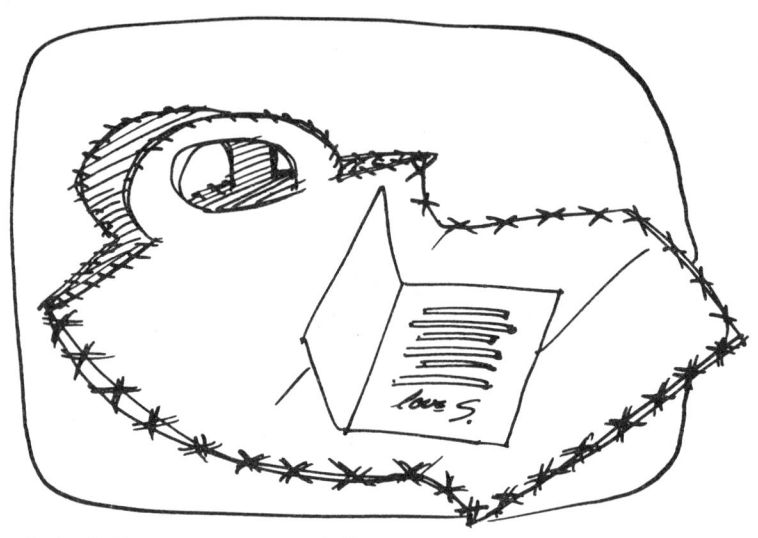

14 Moments with Christmas Poetry

Sometimes it seems hard to sit down and take time for a few minutes of personal enjoyment during the busy holiday season. Yet one of the most relaxing things you can do is to pause to read a little poetry from a favorite Christmas book.

Often there is need for a bit of poetry to open a committee meeting or a church circle program. Copied here are some of my own poems which have been used in such capacities.

DEAR LITTLE CHURCH

Church of my youthful heart, I love you still,
Although the busy years have passed by so fast,
Still I can hear the lovely carols of Christmas,
In memory their beautiful words and music last.

Where are the happy friends of the early years,
Who often walked up the steps and sat beside me?
Together we sang of the birth of the baby Jesus,
Promised Son of God to live through all eternity.

Grateful we are, dear little church of yesterday,
That you stood on the tree-shaded corner near home,
Your message of God's great gift at Christmastime
Remains a true blessing wherever our feet may roam.

CHRISTMAS ROSE

Once I loved the tightly furled bud of a rose,
And mourned to see its petals open and fall.
Now I seek out the full-blown Christmas rose,
Loving its fulfilled beauty the best of all.

For I have found that only by opening the heart
Can life's true meaning ever really be known,
And by facing outward with family and friends
Daily joys and Christmas blessings have grown.

THE ROAD TO CHRISTMAS

When shepherds watched their flocks by night,
How beautiful it must have been to sight the star.
No wonder they followed swiftly to find the Child,
Where hope beckons in beauty the road is not far.

CHRISTMAS CANDLE

Tonight when I saw a candle burning in your window,
Beside a holly wreath, I wondered if you knew, dear,
That your friendship shines as brightly as that taper,
Sending its lovely light down my pathway all the year.

CHRISTMAS RENEWED

I missed Christmas last year
   (Though I lived through December)
Where Christmas went and how
   Is what I'm trying to remember.

Toys and trees aglint with tinsel,
   Hosts of busy shoppers I recall,
But beyond these, Christmas seems
   Not to have touched me at all.

For hurry is left in my heart,
   Worries I carry day by day,
For these there would be no room
   Had Christmas come to stay.

So hear my thanks, Dear Father,
   That Christmas comes each year,
With another chance for me to accept
   Christ's ever present love so dear.

A PROJECT FOR HOME JOY

Many lovely poems come on Christmas cards or in booklets. Do not lose these after the holiday season, but place them in a special Christmas Bag. Take a piece of green felt, approximately 12 inches by 24 inches, and fold it in the center. Stitch it along the sides with red yarn. Make a handle of the felt, or crochet the yarn into a handle. Put the booklets and cards inside, and pack the felt bag away with your Christmas decorations. Then it can be taken out next season when you begin your decorations, and your days can be more relaxed if you take time to read the poems. From them come fresh energies and holiday ideas.

PREPARE YOUR HEART FOR CHRISTMAS

Loving Father, so often our days seem so prosaic, lacking the joy and exuberance of poetry. Help us to see that especially at the Christmas season we have a fresh opportunity to put the enthusiasm and energy of beauty back into our lives. Grant that we may not become so burdened with the duties of each day that we fail to take time to lift our eyes toward heavenly skies to enjoy their beauty. In the rhythm of the holiday season may we feel thy presence enfolding us with loving support for joyous days.

15 The Facts of Christmas

When I walked into the home of young friends, the little boy of the family took me by the hand and led me over to the fireplace mantel. He pointed upward and stood on tiptoe, but he was too small to see the decorations.

His father picked the lad up in his arms so he was on eye level with me, while the little boy pointed to an opened book. On his face was a happy smile as he told me with obvious pride a big word he had just learned. *"The Bible,"* he said with firm tones.

It was true, the family Bible was opened and around its pages was fragrant decoration in the form of cedar branches, cut from the lower limbs of the family Christmas tree. A red bookmark indicated the place where the Bible had been opened.

As I leaned forward to make sure of the passage, I was pleased to see that it was my own favorite Christmas reference, Luke 2:1-20. These verses I have

The Facts of Christmas

read aloud in concluding many Christmas programs across my years of writing devotional books.

Now the little boy was excitedly showing me the bookmark he had made to mark this special place, and the moment was made especially precious for me as his attractive young mother joined the circle, with baby sister in her arms. She told the boy he could take out the bookmark and let me see it more closely, and he did so with obvious pride.

He handed me an eight-inch length of red satin ribbon about an inch wide. On it he had pasted seals which had come into the home through the American Bible Society's annual Christmas letter. Some of them were a little askew, but they all reflected the boy's pleasure in being allowed to lick the stamps and put them on the ribbon.

Even as I praised this remarkable bookmark, he reached for it with chubby hands and put it back into the Bible, opened at the Christmas story.

His mother told me then why the family had made this arrangement, and stressed the bookmark. "I want my children to always be aware of the facts of Christmas," she told me with refreshing honesty. "There are so many legends, and ways to get confused, especially when you are little. I want them to remember that we kept the Bible open to the facts of the original Christmas."

The little scene had brought home to me forcefully my own need to remind myself of the simple facts of the first Christmas, since each year the productions and books clustering around the season become more lavish.

I asked the young mother if she could arrange for a baby sitter and come as my guest to a special December meeting of the women of my church. This meeting also focuses on "the facts of Christmas" and tries to stress simplicity. It is called the Christmas Rose Breakfast, and in our part of the country there are usually roses from gardens which can be used for decoration on the tables. Sometimes the roses are made of crepe paper and serve as souvenirs, or the centerpieces are sent as gifts to shut-ins. The program is based on music honoring the Christ Child.

For many years I have been asked to give the opening invocation, which varies with the events of the particular year, but is based on emphasizing the true meaning of the original Christmas. Other women have asked me for copies to use in their churches, and printed here is one written for a recent year.

INVOCATION FOR A CHRISTMAS MEETING

Our dear, kind, loving heavenly Father, as Christmas comes once more, we give thee our praise. Even as we thank thee for the many blessings of the year, we are aware of those who are suffering physical and emotional losses through devastation by fire, flood, and earthquake. May right action be ordered in their lives, and in our own, so that we may serve thee with faithfulness, and our neighbors with compassion. We pray also for our beloved country that in these years of transition we may move forward with peace in our hearts. May there be peace in the world so that all thy children may live in freedom. Give us fresh energy for the happy tasks of this season, as we ask thy blessing on food and fellowship. May we remember that Christmas is the reconciling of God and man through the coming of thy Son, Jesus Christ, our Lord and our Saviour, in whose name we pray. Amen.

The Facts of Christmas

A PROJECT FOR HOME JOY

Make sure there is a sacred corner in your home where you can display the opened Bible, using whatever is your favorite scriptural passage describing the first Christmas. Put this in place at the first of December, and as the month progresses, put different Christmas objects beside it. Sometimes I use a very special card which has come in from a distant country where a friend now lives. Seeing it as a bookmark makes the friend seem closer to me this blessed season. Or it may be that a child brings a crayon picture of a Christmas tree, which can be propped up behind the opened Bible. Maybe a special flower blooms, reminding of a loved one, and this bloom may pay special tribute beside the scripture.

PREPARE YOUR HEART FOR CHRISTMAS

Father, we are grateful for the enduring words of the Bible so that the beloved Christmas story can be told to us in the space age. Help us remember the facts of Christmas, and keep them uppermost in our planning in our homes, clubs, churches, and communities. May our actions be undergirded by love of others and respect for ourselves as thy children and with thy Son, Jesus, as our Brother. Grant to thy beautiful world the blessings of thy eternal peace as promised at the first Christmas, and may it begin in each heart.

16 The Heart-Trimmed Tree

When the orange-red flames swept down from the mountainside they carried all the young growing Christmas trees with them. The fire also destroyed the home of good friends of ours, whose small daughter is very dear to our hearts.

So on the afternoon before Christmas we went in search of the rented house they had found as living quarters while the debris was being removed from what had been the garden of their lovely home.

As we rang the doorbell, we glanced through the window and saw a small green tree. It was festooned with chains made from red and green construction paper. But what were the golden decorations? When we got inside we saw these were hearts, made from gold paper.

The little girl hugged us both as my husband and I handed her a tiny package. She said, "Oh, you've brought me something for my tree. And I made these hearts myself."

The Heart-Trimmed Tree

Even as we admired them, the mother said, "It was her idea. For everything we have to decorate this tree has been brought to us by people who had it in their hearts to help us forget the fire and the burning of our long-treasured decorations."

We commented on how sad it was to lose favorite possessions, and how much we admired their courage in the face of loss. The father said, "Really this is turning out to be a happy Christmas. Nobody was burned in the fire, we are all safe, and we can start over together in the New Year."

The little girl insisted that we take a closer look at the tree from which the golden hearts were dangling in profusion. She showed us candy canes, a gingerbread man, a cookie star, a popcorn ball, and a veritable rainbow of satin ornaments with silver sequins.

As we looked, she babbled along, telling us the names of the neighbors and friends who had contributed the decorations. She held in her hand the lightweight package we had given her, and she asked us to help her loop the ribbon over a low-hanging limb. She wanted this on the tree, so she could open it Christmas morning.

She wondered out loud what could be in such a lightweight package that it could hang on a tree. We told her this was a secret until Christmas morning, but hoped that she would be pleased when she did open it. For we had found a cornhusk doll with a gay pink sunbonnet to add to her collection. The doll also had a pink ribbon sash, and, knowing our small friend, we felt she might find a way later to tie the doll itself to her heart-trimmed tree.

Sure enough, her thank-you note said: "Thank you for the doll. I hung it on the tree. It was so pretty that now I am going to hang it in my room. That way I will always keep it hanging in my heart."

I read and re-read the letter, because its last phrase seemed so meaningful. The little girl had shown me clearly once again the real purpose of all Christmas gifts. She had said she would always keep the gift in her heart.

Isn't that the real reason any of us try to find gifts for those we love—so that our gesture may be kept in their hearts? Isn't the real meaning of Christmas the fact that Christ came to live in our hearts, as a reminder of the love of God?

The child's perceptive note of thanks about the doll from the heart-trimmed tree has reminded me anew of the great gift of the Christmas Child.

It has caused me to take a good look at my own actions in the Christmas season. Have I become selfish in my giving? Is my list for friends and relatives the only list that concerns me?

Do I work so hard at finding unusual gifts that I do not have energy to think about the community agencies which minister to needy children? Are my funds truly budgeted from the heart, or from well-defined pathways of the past?

Heart-trimmed trees are needed by many community agencies, and if each of us could give just one gift, the combined total would prove significant in ministering to human needs.

A PROJECT FOR HOME JOY

Take a good look at your gift list. How many gifts are based on heartfelt needs? Do you know the heart of your nearest and dearest well enough to know what he or she really and truly wants for Christmas? It may be a gift of time, instead of money or something bought with money. Perhaps it is a wish for a more solvent budget, and your cutting down on spending would be the best gift a husband or wife could have this season. Does a gift come from your "head" in practical measure, or is it time you made a frivolous purchase of some silly item you know a loved one truly desires in the heart? The child who had a heart-trimmed tree has helped me make my own gift list more personal and heartwarming to the recipient.

PREPARE YOUR HEART FOR CHRISTMAS

Father, may we be enabled to see with the eyes of the heart, and truly come to know the needs of those who are closest to us. Forbid that we should keep a wall between us and our dear ones, and may Christmas be a season when we learn anew to share from our hearts. If this means asking for forgiveness for taking others for granted, may we have the grace to humble ourselves. Give us guidance in the selecting of gifts, so that they will truly express the loving concern of our hearts and undergird our dear ones with daily affection.

17 Christmas Bazaar Blessings

When I was a little girl, my mother would invite me to go with her to the Christmas bazaar at our church. One of my earliest memories is of sitting in a little green chair over in the corner by the Christmas tree and eating a cookie in the shape of a gingerbread man. What should I save for the last—his legs, arms, head, or peppermint candy buttons?

Meanwhile my mother was involved with other decisions. Should she spend her carefully hoarded funds from the grocery money on hand-crocheted potholders, dish towels with flowers embroidered in the corner, or coathangers with knitted protectors over the wooden forms?

It was exciting to look over her purchases and then help her wrap them in white tissue and tie them with red or green yarn. Perhaps because of this happy memory, I still delight in attending church bazaars.

Last year I had an encounter which gave me a wonderful spiritual gift that has lasted all through the year. As I entered the festooned room, I saw an elderly lady who had been one of my mother's youngest friends in earlier days. She was sitting alone in an overstuffed chair by the Christmas tree, even as I used to sit there in the tiny one. Her hands were folded in her lap.

I could remember when she would have been busy bustling around the booth where doughnuts were being fried in sizzling grease. Then she would have given a quick twist of her wrist, and rolled them in powdered sugar, and put them into a waxed paper holder. Mother would have bought me one, and I might have gone outside to eat it with my playmates.

Now the former doughnut maker sat alone, and I went over to join her. She took my hand and pulled me down on the couch near her chair, and stroked my fingers with her own gnarled ones. Sadly she said to me, "This is the first year I have not been able to at least crochet potholders for the handiwork table."

I told her how much I enjoyed the lovely handwork she had made in other years, and how I used it daily in my home when taking hot dishes from the oven. My friend continued, "I didn't even want to come this year, as it is so hard for me to face people since my husband died last summer."

Humbly I patted her hand and said that we all knew how she felt. "We all miss him," I told her; "he always had so much fun in that red and white Santa Claus suit you made for him." She wiped a tear from her eye, and said, "No, I didn't want to come at all, but my daughter and her family need some time alone, and when her husband offered to bring me, I decided to come. I'm going to stay here all day, and let them have a little vacation to themselves. I'll look at the pretty things others have made, and they tell me I can buy a sandwich for lunch."

I told her she would also be seeing friends who loved her, and asked if I could sit with her a while longer. Together we watched a young mother go by, holding by the hand her little girl as together they searched for the proper cloth doll. We saw two little boys deciding which marbles to pick up at the odds-and-ends table and take to the cashier.

A teacher stopped by to show us the little worship center she had bought for her work desk. It resembled a miniature colorful window, and had been made by cutting a hole in the side of a blue plastic bottle. At the base had been added little bits of plastic greenery and a red ceramic bird.

We remarked on how interesting it was that, with a little imagination and ingenuity, even a kitchen container could be turned into an item for a Christmas bazaar.

"Yes," said my wise older friend. "All these years we have always brought what we could make from what we had." She sighed and said, "But this year all I could bring was myself."

Looking at her sweet face, I knew she had brought the best gift of all. "Never think that you have nothing to give," I told her, "for I have already received from you today the great gift of courage." As I went in search of a drink and cookies for us both, I was aware of the many kinds of Christmas bazaar blessings.

A PROJECT FOR HOME JOY

Determine that this will be the year when you make some contribution to your church bazaar which will be fun for you as well as a source of help for someone else. One year I saved stationery boxes—those with sturdy bottoms and transparent tops. I lined the boxes with waxpaper, and put candies where the stationery had been. The see-through top enabled the customer to tell at a glance that this was indeed fudge or divinity, and hastened sales. Little is needed in the way of other wrapping, although a red ribbon with a piece of greenery is easy and attractive.

PREPARE YOUR HEART FOR CHRISTMAS

Dear God, in the preparation for Christmas through such activities as our church bazaars, it is so easy to lose sight of the need to prepare our own hearts to receive fresh gifts. May we find, in the fellowship with others, a new encouragement for friendly actions throughout the year. May we never become too busy to stop to chat with those who are lonely as the years bring their inevitable changes. In the great bazaar of life may our hearts make wise choices, that we may serve thee better.

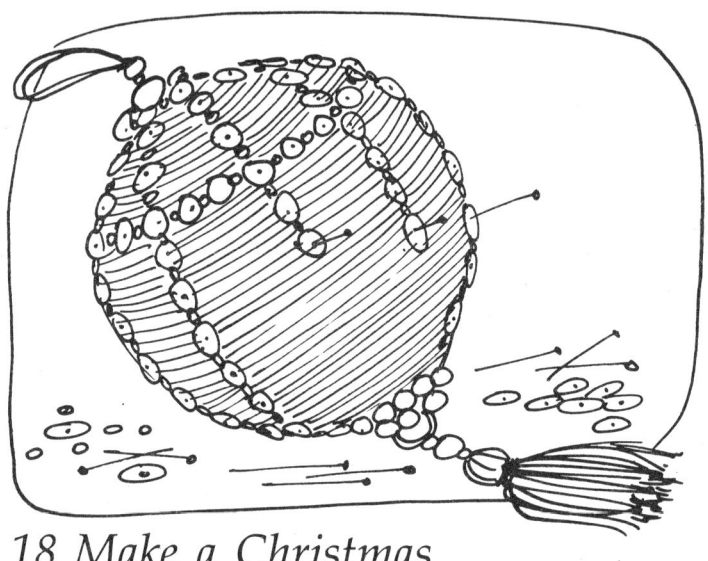

18 Make a Christmas Heirloom

One of the nicest ways to get ready for Christmas is to spend some free moments during the year working on "a Christmas heirloom." Most of us today do not have much leisure time, but if there is a project to which we can turn for relaxation, often stress can be lessened in the daily routine.

In our home we found this to be true the year we worked on a sampler which said "Joy to the World." This Christmas needlework was in the form of cross-stitch. We had not designed it ourselves, but purchased it through a needlework catalogue. We find that cross-stitch happens to be a hobby we enjoy with our hands, and that just a few stitches taken in a five- or ten-minute span of time can create and finish a piece over the course of a year.

So as we worked on a Christmas heirloom, we were aware of the blessings of friendship expressed in cards at the holiday season. And we had in our consciousness also the great gift of Christmas itself, a reminder of the

Make a Christmas Heirloom

coming of Jesus into the world as Saviour and Prince of Peace.

The directions for working the Joy to the World sampler said to use red thread for the words of the familiar phrase, and two shades of green for the boughs and branches at the top of the piece. Some brownish gold or bronze embroidery thread was provided for four bells, suspended by red banners, but we wanted to make them of golden metallic thread.

Eventually we found where to purchase this, so we could make the four bells look like the Golden Bells for Christmas. Working them was a special joy as they reminded us of the bells and chimes in church steeples which we have heard in various parts of the world, announcing the arrival of the Christ through the beloved Christmas carols.

When the handwork was finished, we carefully pressed the embroidered material and then went in search of a golden frame. This set apart the bells, and seemed to emphasize the joyous and reverent words with which many of us welcome Christmas by singing "Joy to the World."

The first year we placed the picture near the doorway to our home, and when the holiday was over we took it down and packed it away with our "decorations" and put back in place the nature picture.

The heirloom we had made had already added much pleasure in its first year in service in our home. The next year we brought it out again and moved it into the family room. We found that friends came into our home looking for it as a part of our decorations.

When the season was over, we decided to keep it up in place. Throughout the year, the words of Christmas passed into our subconscious minds every time we passed the sampler. Often in some moment of emotion or crisis, seeing the sampler seemed to bring fresh peace into our minds and relax us for current tasks.

We were grateful that the odd moments for needlework had been expended on this piece, which was proving a fruitful blessing throughout the year. This encouraged us to look for other items which we could make in future years.

The next project proved to be a Christmas tablecloth, also done in cross-stitch and taken from a catalogue. The pattern had holly wreaths scattered throughout the cloth, each tied with a simple cross-stitched red bowknot. Because only the two colors were used against the white it was not mind-taxing to try to concentrate on choosing elaborate colors of many shades, as is often true in tablecloth patterns. It proved relaxing to pick up either green or red thread, and put in stitches.

Then we could visualize the family gathered around the festive cloth for the Christmas dinner. Because it was embroidered on drip-dry material, it could be washed easily and made ready for another meal with friends or a children's party.

A third year we worked on another tablecloth, specifically with children in mind, for we found a pattern featuring several motifs popular at Christmas. These included a candy cane, a top, a tiny tree, and an ornament. This helped us plan ahead for treats with neighborhood children.

The making of a Christmas heirloom now provides year-round pleasure as a handiwork hobby.

A PROJECT FOR HOME JOY

Spend some time analyzing what kind of handiwork you really prefer to do in your limited spare time. Do you like to work with sequins? Then you can create a remarkable assortment of tree ornaments made from styrofoam balls and sequins put in place by pins. Would you rather work with felt? Then select from the assortment of Christmas tree "skirts" provided for the base of a tree. Some of these are meant to be embroidered with yarn, and others are appliqued with other shades of felt. Would you rather do a wall banner with the three wise men? Pamper yourself in choosing a design to give pleasure through the year, and then apply the moments of stress or discouragement to positive working out of tension through handiwork.

PREPARE YOUR HEART FOR CHRISTMAS

Father, we do not wish to lose the feeling of grace coming from the Christmas season, but would like to keep it alive in our hearts through the routine days of the year. Keep us mindful of the central message of Christmas, the coming of Joy to the World. Help us learn better how to express this joy in our homes, churches, clubs, and communities. May the Christmas season remain in our hearts as we use our hands to perpetuate the precious meaning of the season, expressing our talents in reverence and beauty.

19 Holiday Decorating of the Ordinary

A newcomer to our area telephoned early in December and asked me if I could stop by to see her Christmas decorations. She said she had really had a good time as she had tried to "just spruce up the ordinary for the holidays."

Moving cross country the box of Christmas decorations had somehow been lost or left behind. Her budget did not permit her to go out and buy a lot of new decorations, and she was homesick, so she got busy to use what she had in getting ready for the holiday in a new area.

She had met me at a church program and wondered if I would stop by, for she missed her friends from home. As I looked at the Christmasy decorations, I began to feel more like observing the holiday myself and told her so.

She said, "I started with just what we use everyday, and I am so glad if you think the house looks pretty."

She showed me how she had placed some greenery

Holiday Decorating of the Ordinary

behind a nature picture in the hallway. The fresh shrubbery had brought out the greens in the picture in a way in which she had never seen them before.

As we studied the picture she said, "I always thought of it as a study in blues and golds, and I brought it from home because I've lived with it for a long time and it is like a familiar friend." Now, using the fresh shrubbery from her new home, she had a new appreciation of beauties before unseen in the picture.

In a white vase on the mantel she had placed some red geraniums, and the effect was striking in its bold simplicity. Coming from a colder climate, she had been intrigued by how well the common geranium grew in this area and had found a way to highlight it in her new home, an example to those of us who had come to take the flower for granted.

She told me she had usually used an arrangement of colored balls in a silver bowl, but she did not wish to buy such replacements now in case the missing decorations finally turned up with the misplaced moving boxes.

Hoping for mail from home, she had turned a metal wastebasket into a lovely receptacle for Christmas mail by the simple expedient of wrapping around it a bright red bath towel. She had pinned this in place with a coat ornament made from green felt cut in the shape of a Christmas tree and sewn to a large safety pin.

Because the embroidered and sequined stockings the family usually hung at the fireplace were still missing, she had settled for two pairs of red socks, purchased at the notions counter in the nearest supermarket. They reminded her of the more simple Christmases of her childhood, and all the family were enjoying the socks, and planning tiny surprises to go inside.

Instead of the red net cloth which usually went over the dining table at Christmas, she was using her regular tablecloth. The two children had cut out figures from magazines to paste on three-by-five-inch cards, cut in half, to use as placecards.

A Santa Claus from an advertisement had been mounted on cardboard for stiffness and placed on the side table beside the bowl of hard candies, as if inviting guests to help themselves.

As I took a chair near the candies, she urged me to have some. Together we sat in the cozy living room, exchanging Christmas chit-chat and talking about food for the holidays.

I told her how much I admired her ingenuity in using what she had and making it seem fresh and inviting, and said I would try to put some of the ideas into practice when I got home.

She asked me about what was available in the way of entertainment, especially for her children, in this new area, and I told her about the decorations at the mall. By her question she had made me see that what I took for granted in my hometown was indeed a special treat for someone who had come from a distance and was trying to get acquainted.

With gratitude I thanked my new young friend for inviting me to stop by her home, for she had shown me that loving care of the ordinary could turn it into the extraordinary, not only at Christmas but throughout the year.

A PROJECT FOR HOME JOY

Start with the front doorway of your home and see what the family can do to make it look different at the holiday time than it does the rest of the year. Some people like to make a wreath of greenery, which is always a pretty accessory; but a few boughs tied together with a red ribbon and placed on a doorknob make a quick and easy substitute. One year we hung strings of bright beads, unearthed from a forgotten jewelry box, draping them over the porch light, and letting the light shine through the various colors of the beads. On a string of pinecones we tied a half dozen red and blue Christmas balls, and let the light reflect from them for another holiday welcome.

PREPARE YOUR HEART FOR CHRISTMAS

Dear God, please forgive us for taking the ordinary things of our lives so much for granted that we even become tired of them through the years. Let Christmas be a time when we take a new look at what is ours to enjoy in the way of furniture, art, dishes, books. May we never become so surfeited with things that we crave even more. Rather give us eyes to see new ways to use that to which we have become accustomed. Let the holidays add a sense of zest to our daily routines and possessions so that life seems brighter and better.

20 Celebrate with Christmas Cupcakes

A young bride said to me last Christmas, "I wish I could bake gifts in my kitchen, but the rest of you cook so well I am afraid to try."

I tried to remind her that the best cook had to learn at some time, and she didn't need to be so fearful. Besides, one of the easiest ways to begin with gifts from the kitchen is to celebrate with Christmas cupcakes.

She asked me where to start, and I confessed to her that early in December my shopping list always includes several packages of prepared cake mixes. And I try never to forget to pick up some of the little paper cups to place in muffin tins to serve as cupcake containers, and which can also be a part of the gift wrapping of the present from the kitchen.

Choose any cake mix you prefer: white, yellow, chocolate, or any of the fruit flavors, including the reddish cherry mix, which reminds of the holiday. Directions are always on the package for how to mix the dry ingredients with either water, milk or eggs.

Celebrate with Christmas Cupcakes

If you choose white cake mix, make also a simple white icing, so you have "snow cakes." Sprinkle over them some of the white sparkling candies often used on birthday cakes. Label the cakes by writing your choice of names on the tag which goes on the white paper plate on which they can be given to a friend.

You can vary the appearance by using white icing and adding some cinnamon candies, which will resemble holly berries. Add some green coloring matter to part of the white icing mix, and use droplets of this green confection as "leaves" next to the red-hots. Or ice the cake in green completely, and arrange the red-hots in larger numbers so they look like the petals of a poinsettia.

Inexpensive paper figurines are available from import shops, and these come attached to toothpicks that can be stuck into the tops of the cakes. Thus a Christmas assortment can include angels, Santa Claus, stars, little elves, and miniature trees.

Candy-cane Christmas cupcakes are attractive. Buy the tiniest confection canes you can find, and either stick the end into the center of the cake, so the cane stands up like a handle, or else place it down flat on top of the cake.

Make snowmen out of marshmallows and let them sit in the snow of the white frosting. By using two sizes of marshmallows and holding them together with toothpicks you can fashion a reasonable facsimile of a snowman, which children especially will enjoy.

Naturally cakes which have snowmen, or candy canes which stand upright, cannot be packed easily in boxes as gifts. They are more desirable for use at your own family table, where they add a festive touch at small cost.

If you wish to pack cakes to send away, use tiny candies or "confection glitter" which can be sprinkled on top of the icing. Line an old Christmas card box with waxed paper and put the tiny cakes on the bottom; then cover with another layer of the waxed paper. Use a paper lid for top, instead of the see-through kind. The minute the lid is removed, the attractive cakes can be seen through the waxed paper. They provide their own decoration and speak immediately of Christmas good eating.

Another way to pack cupcakes is to wrap each one in a sandwich bag. Then place the bags in the box, touching each other so they do not jostle in the mail. Thus protected by the sandwich bags, the cakes keep a special freshness.

If the cakes are intended for nearby friends or neighbors they do not need to go in a box. Wrap them in the sandwich bags and place half a dozen on a sheet of heavy foil. Cut the foil wide enough and long enough to fold back over the top and sides of the six cakes. Then fasten it with clear tape. Add a bright poinsettia paper napkin, or one with a picture of Santa Claus, over the top, fastening it with tape. Then tie a piece of red yarn around the package.

This is a variation from the paper plate as a tray, and the package is always attractive when you put a Christmas paper napkin beneath the cakes. It's easy to begin your holiday baking fun when you celebrate with Christmas cupcakes.

A PROJECT FOR HOME JOY

Determine to follow through on your desire to learn how to do Christmas baking. Once you make the effort, it becomes easier year after year, and it is a fine way to build self-confidence in the kitchen. Add spice and flavor to your baking by using whatever is most available in your own area. Do you live where there are black walnut trees? Walnuts add a special flavor to Christmas baking. If instead you live where English walnuts are prevalent, learn how to use them for stuffing dates or adding to fudge. Study the cookbooks often put out free of charge by those who sell such products as molasses, coconut, and brown sugar. Become an expert in some special field by learning what you can about a food product which will dress up your daily menus as well as holiday baking.

PREPARE YOUR HEART FOR CHRISTMAS

Dear Father, we thank thee for the abundance of natural foods which are a part of thy great world. Bless this day those who serve in far-off corners of the world, remote from our homes, but who come into our kitchens through the fragrant spices we use in our cooking. Enlarge our vision of the world as we use the grains for bread, and the flavorings for our puddings and sauces. Help us remember that we are a part of one another in this world of thy creation, and that we must learn to live as brothers and sisters in peace and harmony.

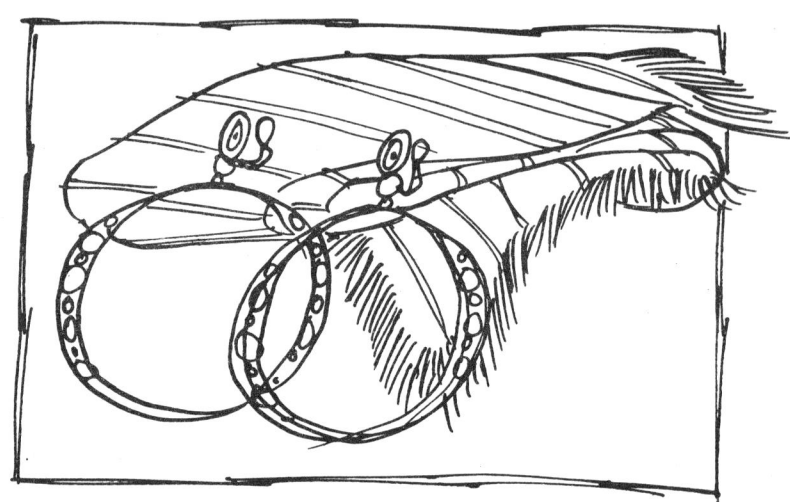

21 Something *New* for Christmas

When a little boy was given a pair of new shoes for Christmas his face broke into a beautiful smile. "Something NEW for Christmas was what I wanted," he told the service club representative who had been assigned to take clothes to this single-parent family.

The businessman who told me the story said he had gone with some trepidation, feeling the child would want a toy instead, and that shoes seemed so prosaic a gift.

"I learned something that day," he told me. "There is nothing that means quite so much as having something NEW."

Most of us forget this in our busy days, taking for granted the new clothes we are able to buy. But the novelty and rareness of "newness" is a rich treasure to those who for one reason or another become used to wearing hand-me-downs. This is true currently not only for children in homes broken by divorce where a single parent battles inflation with a small salary, but

Something *New* for Christmas

also for many retired persons who formerly had opportunity to buy new garments.

When I spoke of this to a friend who counsels those in trouble, she said to me, "It gives a person, whether child or adult, a fresh sense of confidence whenever a gift is brand new." And the feeling of self-respect is one of the first ideals on which character can be developed.

Putting this philosophy into practice can add much joy to community observances of Christmas in gifts to organizations serving others. It has carry-over value for those who participate in the giving, for it reminds them that Christmas itself comes each year with a joyous sense of newness about it.

The sacred season puts a stamp of newness on old friendships, and rejuvenates business relationships by causing people to take a fresh look at those whom they meet throughout the year. There is opportunity to transform the routine of daily acts into rituals of loving seasonal enjoyment. Something "new" for Christmas may well be a renewed spirit of awareness and enjoyment of others throughout the busy new year of service.

One tangible result of such a spirit was the project begun by an association which serves men and women confined to rest homes. The board decided to take a new look at its Christmas practices and see what it was that the residents really needed and wanted most.

One of the nurses provided the clue when she told of one woman who was so sad because she could no longer shop for loved ones in her family. She had asked the busy nurse if she would pick up a little bottle of hand lotion which she could give to her granddaughter at the holiday season. The nurse was too busy to do this for many of the patients, but when she told the association about the need, a plan was devised whereby each member agreed to bring a gift which

A Heart-Trimmed Christmas

some man or woman in the convalescent home could in turn give away to a dear one.

By thus dividing the tasks, the shopping was not difficult for anyone. Gifts which came to the meeting in the hands of members included not only the hand lotion, but small bottles of toilet water or shaving lotion, notepads, writing paper, tiny figurines, and small vases with plastic flowers.

A committee wrapped these volunteer gifts, marking them for either a man or a woman. Through the office the chairman received a list of the names of the patients, and learned whether a son or daughter was the one responsible for the parent. Thus it was easy to pick out a gift for a man or woman and add the name of the recipient, plus the name of the patient who was the giver.

The pleased expression on the faces of those who received the gifts was matched by the satisfaction of the patients who were thus enabled to make a gift. And this happiness was reflected back onto the members of the organization who devised the new plan for Christmas remembrances.

The something NEW for Christmas had resulted in greater fellowship and an increased awareness of daily blessings, such as the ability to walk into a store and buy an object. The jaded attitude toward shopping chores was lost in a new awareness of others and their human needs for recognition and the joy of sharing.

A PROJECT FOR HOME JOY

Take a good look around your home and see what there is that is new that you can share with others this holiday season. At first glance, this may seem an impossible request, but most of us tuck things away in drawers and forget about them, unless motivated to seek them out.

The season I tried this plan, I found two new scarves, which were the wrong length for me but which proved exactly right for two women in a convalescent home, who wanted extra warmth around their shoulders when sitting near the air conditioner in summer. A look at the jewelry drawer unearthed large, hooped-shaped golden earrings, which delighted a young friend with a gypsy spirit and which would never have matched my more sedate tastes. Share the new you have and do not hoard it; thus joy is multiplied.

PREPARE YOUR HEART FOR CHRISTMAS

Dear God, we ask forgiveness for taking our blessings for granted, and becoming dull in our approach to the holidays. Grant to us the fresh zest of newness which children feel as the holiday approaches, but let us remember that not all children can feel this completely because of lack of family funds. Help us become part of the group who seek for the answer in providing joy for such children by furnishing new clothing or toys. May we keep this new attitude of caring alive in our hearts through daily routines.

22 Christmas Correspondence

Each year the matter of tending to Christmas correspondence becomes somewhat of a problem in many homes, particularly with increasing costs of cards and postage. One of my friends confessed, "Just when I start to cut my list, I realize that I need my friends more than ever, so the list usually grows."

She is not alone in this decision, and so the custom of Christmas cards continues. Various are the methods used by friends to display the cards which arrive in the mail.

Some tape them against the fireplace mantel, hang them around the doorway, or put them in a fancy golden basket or a big red stocking. All seem to have special decorative touches to add to Christmas festivity.

One busy season when I did not use my cards for decoration, but merely stacked them in a pile, I really enjoyed them more than before. I discovered in careful reading that I had been missing much that was coming to me on cards, for my friends seem to have a real talent for hiding messages on the backs of cards, or up in the corner below the mistletoe, or in a wide triangle at the bottom of the middle fold.

Sometimes the cards contain a mimeographed letter, too long to read during the before-Christmas rush but which can be savored in later reading and relishing. I cherished especially such a letter which said, "Even though the facts we give you contain some sad news, we want you to know how much our friends do mean to us at this season, and that we are glad we can share our experiences with you by this card."

Here were friends who were facing up to the difficulties of the past year and reaching out to their friends, instead of withdrawing. Such retreat almost always leads inevitably to self-pity, the most debilitating of emotions. Reaching out, on the contrary, offers hope of catching on to new experiences.

Sometimes it is difficult to know how to respond to such news in Christmas letters. We recall the note from a young man whom we had long admired, and whose wife we had enjoyed meeting when he came proudly to introduce her to us.

We opened the letter expecting good news, but found the incredible word that they were divorced. "We were married ten years and they were such happy years for me," he wrote. "I never dreamed she wanted out until the very day she left." He said the divorce had occurred early in the year, but he could not bear to write us until now and did so only because he wanted us to have his apartment address and did not want to lose touch with us at Christmastime.

In the same mail was a note from older friends telling us of the loss of their daughter, who had a special way of dealing with young children who had problems in learning as quickly as others in their class. This young woman had a physical disability which had kept her at home in her early years but had given her a patience which enabled her to help others. Now the parents wrote that she had died within the year. "We are almost inconsolable," they told us, "because at last she seemed to be getting stronger. Just when we were least expecting it she is gone from us, and this is a lonely Christmas."

A third letter came from a young family with their first child, to whom we had sent a "first book" made of cloth, telling the Nativity story. They thanked us on their card for what might be in the package which they had safely under the tree. "We thank you for helping give us a Christmas, and please keep on praying that we find work soon." It had not been easy to locate a new job in their new location, made necessary by family health problems.

On Christmas morning I was still thinking about these notes which had come in the holiday mail. Obviously I must send some sort of answer, and I prayed for wisdom in writing return notes. Even when I picked up a pen, holly notepaper, and three envelopes, I did not know what I was going to say.

As I waited for guidance, words came which seemed to fit all three situations, different as they were in outer details. I wrote: "Thank you for telling us of your current situation, and asking us to lift it up to God in prayer. May he grant to you renewed strength and fresh energy for the changed circumstances of your life. May you be a blessing to others each day of the New Year."

As I posted the letters, I realized that the three who wrote had shown me clearly the true opportunities of Christmas correspondence. The season gives us a special time to speak about the emotions closest to our hearts. It allows us to share with those we love in the most intimate of our sorrows and joys. Blessed

Christmas Correspondence

Christmas brings the promise of renewed strength for the New Year.

A PROJECT FOR HOME JOY

Resolve to be generous in sharing the beauty which comes into your home through Christmas cards. If possible find some time between Christmas and New Year's to cut off the signatures and handwritten notes, and put the pictures into a sack to be taken to the nearest community center, veterans hospital, or day-care center. In another bag to save at home, put the mimeographed letters and special notes which call for answers when your schedule permits. If there are foreign stamps, cut them from the envelopes to share with interested children, or give to organizations which sort them for special funds.

PREPARE YOUR HEART FOR CHRISTMAS

Father, we are so often slow in expressing our love for dear ones, and so rushed for time we fail to even sign our names, but use printed greetings. Help us remember there is no gift so great as our own personal signature, made possible by the gift of life and our own special talents from thee. We thank thee for friends who reach out to us, and give us grace to return their trust and faith by clasping outstretched hands. When we must in turn ask for help, give us the ability to lose our pride and be willing to accept Christian encouragement.

23 Silver Holly and Candles

At twilight on Christmas Eve, a car stopped at our driveway, and a lovely friend rang the doorbell. In her hand was a package, wrapped in silver paper and tied with a red ribbon. At the top was attached a single spray of plastic silver holly.

She handed it to me at the doorway and said she could not come inside, as she wanted to get on home while the red and gold sunset was still to be enjoyed.

I understood her unwillingness to be out alone much later, for this was her first Christmas since the death of her fine husband, who had been our friend for many years.

As I looked at the attractive package, she said: "Please open it at once, and use it tonight. Share it with your own husband while you listen to carols, or when you come home from church. It comes with my love and appreciation for all the affection and help I have received from you this difficult year."

When she had gone we removed the holly, ribbon,

Silver Holly and Candles

and paper, and found inside a glorious white candle, four-sided and molded with angels holding musical instruments and a book.

The candle seemed too beautiful to use, but she had asked us to please use it on Christmas Eve, so my husband reached for a china saucer on which to place it, and then for a match to light the wick.

We turned out the lights and let the large candle furnish illumination between us and the lights of our valley, where many homes had candles in the window, according to the old legend of lighting the way for the Christ Child.

As we listened to music from the stereo, with the sound turned low and soft, we reflected on the events of the year and how graciously our friend had received our feeble efforts to help her in her loss.

Now she had reminded us through her gift that "candles are to burn," their purpose is to give light to the surrounding area. They fail of their intention if someone does not light them and place them where they can be enjoyed and used.

So also are we admonished in scripture to let our own light shine, and to receive the light which is available. This calls for learning the happy art of receiving, which is not always an easy thing to do.

I recall how a young man exclaimed to me, "Nothing I do is right when it comes to picking out presents. I'll bet my wife returns this the minute the store opens the day after Christmas."

I had encountered him while on a shopping tour of my own, and sensed his efforts to please, and how already his joy in the gift was dissipated because of his fear that it would not be accepted with grace.

In contrast my own shopping that particular day was the happier because I was choosing a present for a young woman whose squeals of delight I could already

A Heart-Trimmed Christmas

hear in anticipation of her opening the gift. Never had she seemed anything but delighted with any gift given her.

On the previous Christmas, she had received a glamorous pair of lounging pajamas and had that very day worn them, to the delight of her family. When someone protested that she might get them dirty in the kitchen, she said, "Trust me with an apron—and besides, what better time than now to be happy in them?"

No wonder it was fun to buy for this young woman, and how sad it seemed that the wife of the young man I had met had not yet learned this happy art of gracious acceptance.

Knowing that a gift is received with thanks doubles the joy of the giver, and at the same time makes the gift a part of the life of the one who receives.

I admire a young mother who uses her "best" china with her family, although a piece gets broken now and then. "If it is good enough for company, it is good enough for my husband and little boy," she told me. "I receive so much from them, and we ought to be enjoying this together."

Christmas offers us an opportunity to receive with grace. Indeed, the first Christmas cannot be completed until the Saviour is received into the individual heart. In a sense our vows are renewed whenever we accept with joy. I keep the silver holly from the candle package in a little vase in my writing room to remind me to accept the gifts of love at times of sorrow or joy.

A PROJECT FOR HOME JOY

Practice the art of saying "thank you" to those who are nearest and dearest, but who are often the ones who are forgotten. It may be as simple as the one word "thanks," spoken in person or over a long distance telephone call. It can take the form of a simple written note. How I cherish the printing on cards from a little boy with a foreign background, who uses a small letter in writing my name, for he has not yet mastered capital letters. Never does he fail to print his thanks for a book, a pencil, or a seasonal card. His efforts give me fresh energy in the heart both to give and receive.

PREPARE YOUR HEART FOR CHRISTMAS

Father, we are grateful for all such gifts of beauty as the silver holly and the candles, for they come to us out of the depths and heights of our daily living. Help us to see that there are two halves to the perfect gift—the giving and the receiving form an integrated whole. May we learn to give to others, and to receive from them, always letting our light shine to reflect thy goodness. If we have failed to thank thee for the many blessings in our lives, forgive us now, and help us receive more of the life abundant.

24 The After-Christmas Loaf

One of the joys of each Christmas season in our home is the morning when I bake "the after-Christmas loaf." It is never the same two years in succession, and what is baked in our house would not be the same as that baked in your home.

Why? Because the purpose of this special loaf is to incorporate into one delicious baking all the odds and ends left over from the holiday season.

You will be surprised at how good these special leftovers can be in providing a fresh loaf to slice on New Year's Day for munching as the family watches the ball game or entertains drop-in friends.

Start with your favorite quick-bread recipe mix from your own reliable standby recipe. We use the one from a prepared biscuit mix, usually doubling the amount of mix. Thus we add also a little more liquid and maybe an extra egg, so we can include many leftover taste treats in larger loaves.

Next we take all the boxes down from the cupboard

The After-Christmas Loaf

shelves. There is a handful of raisins in the bottom of a box. Maybe in the next box there are a few currants. Use them all now, and if they are a little hard, first soften them in warm water.

Perhaps there are a few walnuts already shelled. If not, take time right now to shell whatever remaining nuts are rolling around in the cupboard. Be sure to add the peanuts in the bottom of the jar left over from the night you had friends in for punch and cookies.

Remember how good the candied orange and grapefruit peel was when a friend brought you some in a foil package? Shake the wrapping well, and use those two or three remaining pieces in the loaf after cutting them to bite size.

Maybe there is a special spoonful or half cup of dried fruits left from the fruitcake recipe. When you made the family traditional cake, you measured exactly; but now you can put in all the dried apricots which are left, or the candied pineapple. You are in luck if there are some candied cherries in the bottom of the jar, for their red adds color.

Shake your spice jars hard, and see if you shouldn't be buying some more cinnamon. It always seems more cinnamon is used at Christmas than any other spice, with the possible exception of ginger.

Empty the nearly empty cans, if there is just a small amount left, and put some spices into your loaf. Then be sure to write down on your grocery list that you need fresh cans of spices to start the New Year cooking.

A little jam or jelly never hurt the after-Christmas loaf, and by all means use up the cranberry sauce. Some orange marmalade adds good flavor, as does that extra dish of applesauce.

You may become so interested that you can't settle for doing this all in one mixing but will want to divide the items and bake twice. We have two large loaf

A Heart-Trimmed Christmas

pans and it is a part of our Christmas tradition to fill them with whatever is this year's current leftover assortment.

How good the house smells as the after-Christmas loaf is baking! We remember the friends who have contributed to it by their gifts. As it bakes, we find our energy rising for taking down the decorations and getting the cards ready to share with those who will use the pictures throughout the year.

By the time your own loaf is baked and cool enough to slice, you may be ready to join in writing thank-you notes for Christmas gifts. It is a good day to get started on the address-book changes in order to prepare for next year's Christmas.

Never overlook in your home the fun of making an after-Christmas loaf, a kitchen summary of all the joys of this current holiday season, as shared with family and friends. You may find it so good that you will want to share it with someone new in your neighborhood, or the old friend you planned to visit but overlooked in the week before Christmas.

A friend to whom I took a portion of our loaf called the visit "a beautiful afterglow to this Christmas season." I found in her spontaneous words one of the rich gifts of my own season. For surely the intent and purpose of all of our holiday preparations is that our loved ones and ourselves may indeed have in our hearts the peace and serenity of the "afterglow" sensed in a beautiful sunset at the close of Christmas Day.

A PROJECT FOR HOME JOY

Choose your own means of winding down from Christmas, if you do not care to make an after-Christmas loaf. Perhaps you are more inclined to really and truly use the lovely new cookbook given by a

The After-Christmas Loaf

friend, or to try out a new piece of kitchen equipment which came as a gift. This may be a gadget for decorating cookies or for making a new design on top of a pie. There is fun in putting into use the new gift items and using what is left in the kitchen from holiday planning. If you have devised a new recipe this season, write it down so you can use it again next year.

PREPARE YOUR HEART FOR CHRISTMAS

Father, we are grateful that Christmas comes each year to remind us anew of the great gift of thy Son. May the blessings of this season remain with us in the days of the year ahead. Give us wisdom and guidance as we put to rest the problems and challenges of this particular year. May we forgive ourselves for our shortcomings, even as we forgive others who may have hurt us in ways past their knowing. May we lose our hurts and our pride in joining in the breaking of bread with family and friends through routine days of service.

25 And a Happy New Year, Too

The week between Christmas and New Year's Day is often a crowded one, with after-Christmas parties, and—let it be confessed—something of an after-Christmas letdown. In good years there is a tendency to linger in the nostalgic glow of the happiness of the season, but in sad ones there is a tendency to get the evidences of Christmas out of the way as quickly as possible.

Most of us have experienced both kinds of the after-Christmas week—the one with afterglow, and the one with aftermath. The week provides a little recess between the sometimes conflicting emotions of the year which is ending, and the one which is beginning.

If it is possible to take a little time to sit down and reflect on the past season, there may appear ideas to help make the Christmas of next year an even better one. One of my friends, who is most methodical, makes a list of activities she considered "good, average, fair, or no good," in trying to become more efficient the next year.

For myself, I find it useful to read some poetry in this interim, and one year I was enabled to put my feelings about this into a poem, which I called

BY ANOTHER WAY

> What other things happened to the Wise Men
> After they had given the Child their treasures?
> Did they go back to face the same old tasks
> Or did life hold for them new pleasures?
>
> Often I had wondered this before I read
> That they returned home by another way.
> May we, too, discover another way to travel,
> Walking love's road after Christmas Day.

Sometimes this intervening week provides an opportunity for us to put into practice some of the ideas we hope to follow through more effectively in the new year. Usually my wishes include the firm desire to be more prompt in my correspondence with old friends, often heard from only once a year, on Christmas cards.

One year I responded to these by including a little verse written after Christmas and called

WISH FOR THE NEW YEAR

> May each minute be long enough for joy,
> And every hour too short for sorrow.
> So may they lengthen into days so happy
> That now will shorten the need for tomorrow.

Often the hopes for the new year involve a determination to take better care of health, so that extras like entertaining will not loom so large an effort and seem to drain physical energy. If reserves can be built up during the routine days of the year, it follows that there will be more of a physical investment to spend and enjoy at happy holidays in another year.

Yet often we procrastinate when we know we should be taking exercise or going for a walk each day. Always it is possible to find excuses, many of them very valid. But the end result is a lack of needed exercise.

If this is true of the physical life, it is even more true in the spiritual realm. We put off establishing a regular time for a prayer life, or for taking time to enjoy the natural beauties of our particular area of the world. Because I live in the Southwest, near the desert, I put my spiritual hopes into a few lines of verse called

NEW YEAR PRAYER FROM THE DESERT

God, help me to remember that tomorrow is like a beautiful mirage,
Ever tempting me onward to look beyond the limits of this very day,
Yet always receding even further into a nebulous distant future,
As weary eyes strain in vain to capture joys glimpsed so far away.

Let me learn, Father, to make the most of each and every new day,
Knowing there is colorful beauty of flowers in desert sand so dry,
And that I am always surrounded by an abundance of life's blessings
Whenever I pause in peace to look for happiness beneath today's sky.

The joy of Christmas and New Year activities is that they do make each day seem special and new. The longer this feeling can be kept alive in the heart, the better will be the whole year.

A PROJECT FOR HOME JOY

Pamper yourself with a few minutes to write down a listing of your favorite dreams. Many books with lovely colors and blank pages are now available for such use. Choose one which appeals to you personally, whether it has roses on the cover, or is a stiff dark blue with gold or silver border. This is for your own enjoyment and should be something you can look at and admire and live with for the year. Be frank with yourself in admitting your needs and hopes. Just seeing them in your handwriting will be an aid to making them come true. Promise yourself some time to yourself to fulfill your own highest potential.

PREPARE YOUR HEART FOR THE NEW YEAR

Dear Father, take the bits and pieces of this last Christmastime and give us the vision to see the lovely pattern which can emerge from our activities with family and friends. Let the memories of the past bless the present, and prepare us for better service in the future. Take from us all evidences of sadness, which hinder our active participation in what is available in the present. Give us fresh courage to carry the routine burdens of each day with cheerfulness, and to work for peace in our hearts and throughout thy great world.